# RUNAWAYS

# RUNAWAYS

A memoir

## Shelley Davidow and
## Shaimaa Khalil

In this memoir certain names and characteristics of people have been changed to protect their identities, and sometimes timelines have been condensed, but the authors have, to the best of their ability, provided an authentic and honest account of their experiences.

Published in 2022 by Ultimo Press,
an imprint of Hardie Grant Publishing

Ultimo Press
Gadigal Country
7, 45 Jones Street
Ultimo, NSW 2007
ultimopress.com.au

Ultimo Press (London)
5th & 6th Floors
52–54 Southwark Street
London SE1 1UN

A catalogue record for this work is available from the National Library of Australia

*Runaways*
ISBN 978 1 76115 064 7 (paperback)

10 9 8 7 6 5 4 3 2 1

**Cover design** Christabella Designs
**Cover image** plataa/Shutterstock
**Typesetting** Kirby Jones | Typeset in 12/16 pt Bembo Std
**Copyeditor** Elena Gomez
**Proofreader** Dženana Vucic
**Author photo** Shelley Davidow courtesy of Emma Adin

Printed in Australia by Griffin Press, part of Ovato, an Accredited ISO AS/NZS 14001 Environmental Management System printer.

The paper this book is printed on is certified against the Forest Stewardship Council® Standards. Griffin Press holds FSC® chain of custody certification SGSHK-COC-005088. FSC® promotes environmentally responsible, socially beneficial and economically viable management of the world's forests.

Ultimo Press acknowledges the Traditional Owners of the country on which we work, the Gadigal people of the Eora nation and the Wurundjeri people of the Kulin nation, and recognises their continuing connection to the land, waters and culture. We pay our respects to their Elders past and present.

For my family.
SD


For Shaza Khalil, Sara El Nemr and Ahmed Zaky: my family,
my soulmates and the keepers of my words.
SK


And for all those whose stories still wait in the silences.
SD and SK

'وطن المرء ليس مكان ولادته ولكنه المكان الذي تنتهي فيه كل محاولاته للهروب،

\*

Home is not where one is born; home is where all one's
attempts to escape cease.

– quote attributed to Omar Taher in *Gar Na'em*

# A NOTE TO THE READER

We grew up a decade apart, girls in Africa's north and south, with that continent's dirt between our toes. Our backgrounds are very different – an Arab Muslim from Egypt, and an Ashkenazi Jew from South Africa – and yet we are connected through certain fragments of DNA. But mostly, we are connected through our hearts, our stories. We met in Doha more than twenty years ago as teacher and student at Qatar University. Both of us new to a strange land, we bonded. In a way we're the most unlikely of pairings but ours has been the most enduring and natural of friendships. In this book, we stitch around the silences, sometimes leaving black holes and voids, hoping to find a place where our female voices are ours, not representative. Between these pages we run away to the end of the world and fall off the edge, off the page. We exchange words and memories, recall what shaped us, what broke us, and we make ourselves whole again through our interwoven story.

Shelley Davidow and Shaimaa Khalil
Australia, 2022

# RUNAWAYS

# 1.

# SHAIMAA

I don't know exactly when my urge to 'run away' became a life's goal. It could've been sometime during my childhood when I found out that my parents were not invincible and that, sooner or later, I would have to make my own way in life. Or maybe it was during puberty when my body and the world turned on me.

Around eight or nine, I started running away in my daydreams, building the places I wanted to be and the person I'd be in them – imagining myself into lightness and liberty, not weighed down by the limitations of gender, culture and society. I began embracing the idea that somewhere in those daydreams I could make my own decisions, and have real agency to determine what to do, what to wear, how to go about my day.

I was jolted by a mix of fear and defeat whenever I heard this from aunties and family elders: 'A good woman leaves her family's house only to live in her husband's house.' God, how shackled I was by this notion – that I had no hope of ever having a whole day on my own, of ever making a decision that was totally mine, of ever having a place that was for me.

*

He (for it is a he, even if his ideas are sometimes embodied and carried out by the women in our lives), wants to control everything: our bodies – ideas – space. I am never just 'I'.

Mine is an ancillary existence to a family and a husband whose honour has been placed on me and a child (preferably more than one) that I have been required to bear.

It's always something else that sanctions my legitimacy in the world.

If the systematic will to kill a spirit and strip a human being of their value and individuality was ever declared a crime as deplorable and punishable as murder, then many women in my region, and arguably the world over, would be survivors of a genocide.

Imagination was the safest place I had and, with it, the power to disappear in broad daylight.

\*

I've become really good at disappearing. At making myself small and invisible. You learn to perfect that if you're a woman growing up in the Middle East. Shelley, you put it so well one time: 'It's like you suddenly turn off your magnetic field.'

For years, I retreated within myself. But that came at a cost I thought I was happy to pay. It came with the repression of thoughts, feelings and self. It came with convincing those fundamental elements of your being that they are not to be shared. Until they stop listening. Until they start a riot and demand to be heard. And how lucky am I that I've had you to share them with.

The heaviness that came with that stifling of self was amplified with the Covid-19 lockdown. We had all these plans to see each other. Shaimaa and Shell, finally in the same country. We pictured weekends in both directions between Sydney and the Sunshine Coast and further trips across Australia. But then it all vanished.

So, we decided to write ourselves back together. What I didn't realise was that I was also writing myself back to myself. Our memories together, our friendship that has endured unforgiving time, geography and major world events. And then something magical happened for me. In the very nightmare of being trapped with looming anxiety attacks, I had something to run away to.

Tonight, I run away
I am weightless
I've shed my mass
I am bigger, better
Enough
Tonight, I run away
I am alone
But not lonely
I create paths
Rise up to challenges
Occupy space
In hearts
In minds
In the world
I let love fill me
I let my being quiver at a first touch
I thread my own story
I become the heroine
I know I could never be
I stand tall
Bask in lightness and flair
Tonight, I run away
I leave the void behind

I wish for nothing to fill it
I don't dream of my child's face
I dare to tell her we won't meet
Tonight, I run away
I look in the mirror
and wonder where I was hiding
I forgo it all
Fear, mediocrity, propriety
that voice that reminds me of all that I'm not
I am not afraid
Tonight, I run away and
I am not afraid

# 2.

# SHELLEY

The university of Qatar was built on the idea, I learned from a colleague, that if a thief came onto the premises, he would get lost. So, classroom 224 might be next door to 136, and 441 might be next to 39. The most stressful part of the day was finding the room I was to teach in. It was in one of these rooms that we met, you and I.

*

1996. I was twenty-seven years old. Paul and I had married and run from Africa to Europe to England looking for work, for a way out of South Africa where jobs were scarce, inflation was rampant and violence was indiscriminately everywhere. After Paul put out more than 300 job applications while we lived in a friend's room in London, the University of Qatar in Doha offered him a position.

Before we left for the Middle East, I dreamt this:

### Before the Desert

Before the windswept shifting sands and plains
Before the silence of the womenfolk,
There was a river – music over rocks
Which fed a fertile valley, rich and green.
When women's voices lifted into song
Their soft vibrating tones loosed water from
High elevations, sent it rushing down
To nourish those who worked the fruitful land.
But then a dry and thankless violent hand
Brought silence down, and water ceased to flow.
Men shouted, fought, trailed murder in their wake
And women's silence as the desert grew
A hundred thousand acres in a year.

Every morning I awoke, and I thought, 'I am in Doha, Qatar, on the Arabian Gulf.' I looked out into the humid, purple-blue air, over dust and rubble towards the Corniche, and beyond that, towards the shallow turquoise waters of the Gulf where once in 1991, according to a rumour, an errant missile sent by Saddam Hussein and meant for Saudi Arabia, had landed. It had exploded, killing fish and making a hole in the soft seabed.

# 3.

# SHAIMAA

The desert was as foreign to me as it probably was to you when you moved to Qatar. Even though I identify as Middle Eastern, North African and Arab – I've never considered the desert as part of my heritage even though my own country has vast swathes of it. When I was in school in Miami, Florida (where my mum had a scholarship to study for a couple of years) and the kids would tease me with the 'walk like an Egyptian' dance and ask if I lived in a tent, I just didn't understand. My notion of home was different. I grew up on the coast ... Alexandria is a small, ancient, vibrant city. A city with centuries worth of stories way before me.

What's funny and slightly disgraceful on my part was that those kids' notion of me back in the US was the one I had of the Gulf when I found out I was moving there. The Gulf was one place to me dominated by three countries that Egyptians went to: Saudi Arabia, Kuwait and the UAE. Qatar was never really mentioned anywhere.

When I landed in Doha in 1996 it was a jolt. I think the most shocking was that this was supposed to be familiar (Arab) territory, but it felt like I'd landed on a different planet.

7

Emptiness ... it dominated. Arid streets, expensive cars, houses with high walls and glass façade buildings paled by dust. People spoke Arabic in a dialect I didn't understand. Not that I saw many Qataris when I landed.

It was 6 pm, and nothing was open. In those days all the shops were closed around that time. A couple of South Asian men were about, and it was the first time I'd ever been looked at like that.

I've grown used to sexual harassment on Egyptian streets, and while the male entitlement to violation was the same, harassment in Doha was different in that there was an element of fascination that a woman dared to step out into the realm of public space where she clearly shouldn't exist. No one was on the streets except the South Asian labourers who would ogle me, my mother and my sister every time we walked down the street.

This was my very first experience in Doha. Walking down the street with my mother to the local supermarket, not really registering the emptiness. My eyes desperately looking for something to be impressed by – to convince myself this was a change for the better.

It would take years for me to find my place in Doha. More years for it to be a second home and eventually another place I'd try to escape.

*

I have a strange relationship with Alexandria – maybe all runaways feel the same, I don't know. But the same things that have carved my hometown inside me have become the very things I wanted to escape. The relative sense of containment and familiarity of a city well past its prime and a little forgotten. The way the streets flooded with the first heavy rainfall every winter. How angry the sea got on those days. The way a street curved and I knew we were close to our house and the shape of the old cabins on the promenade on the way there – small, derelict and eaten by the salty air. God, how I love the smell of salty air! The thrill and utter predictability of a weekend when nothing much happens but at least there's the special breakfast of fava beans, we call it 'foul', falafel and cheese with tomatoes and fresh bread. Then, maybe if we're lucky, a visit to my grandma's house. The smallness of it all. It made me feel safe and suffocated all at once.

I had this thought one day back in Alexandria more than twenty-five years ago. I was out with friends and all I could think was that I wanted to say goodbye to those people, and I wanted them to say goodbye to me.

I wanted to travel and wanted to be away. A few years after that I did travel. And then one year I met you. And that was your story – a story of travel, of leaving places and people and starting anew. I remember thinking, 'I want that to be my story too.'

# 4.

# SHELLEY

When we stepped off the plane in Doha at eight o'clock at night, it was thirty-six degrees Celsius with high humidity. I was wearing black Levi's and the heat hit my body like a wet blanket. The night lit up orange with the glow of the city and I couldn't understand any of the signs or any of the words I was hearing. Men in white thobes flowed around and between the few foreigners. Women in black, tent-shaped, stood or sat near the walls.

There was no line to get through customs. Everything appeared chaotic. I stood behind Paul, jet-lagged and exhausted after the flight from London via Dubai, wondering what on earth we had done, coming here. The air conditioning was freezing.

When the crowd finally allowed us to an immigration window, a man in brusque tones waved Paul on. 'You can go,' he said. 'But your wife, she doesn't have the right visa. She must stay.'

We looked at each other.

Paul had been hired as an English lecturer at the University of Qatar and at the embassy we'd been told only he needed a visa, and our marriage certificate.

Apparently not.

Paul declined the offer of entering the country without me.

There was a conversation between officials that we didn't understand.

Someone stapled a piece of paper to my passport (surely not!) and then our passports were both taken, and we were waved away.

Away.

To wait for we didn't know what.

We waited the whole night.

I cried. 'I want to go back,' I said.

'I know,' Paul said. 'But they have our passports.'

'Why?'

'No idea.'

'Can't we just get on the next plane back to London?'

A futile question.

We were freezing. Paul rummaged through airport bins and found old newspapers. We lay on seats and covered ourselves in sheets of news written in Arabic, to keep ourselves warm, not understanding the words, or why we lay under them.

We were here in Doha, Paul and I, after having first run from South Africa, escaping that violent decaying but beloved country of my birth. Then living in America for three years while Paul got his PhD and eventually running out of a visa, and most recently after London where Paul's British citizenship had allowed us to look for work for nine months, and after finding ourselves with only 300 pounds and no job offerings for either of us after more than 320 applications.

So, when Qatar University offered Paul a lecturing position, we took it with gratitude. It saved us.

\*

11

The next day, following much conversation with officials that made no sense to either of us, we were collected from the airport by two 'university representatives', young men who spoke rudimentary English.

Doha was a strange sight. I felt like I'd landed on the moon. Acres of desert rubble, rocks and stones, a sky orange with dust, a warped red sun that burned through the haze, rows of villas and crazy roundabouts, and a corniche along the shallow blue waters of the Arabian Gulf bordered by high glass buildings – a desert aspiring to be something else.

Our passports were held for three months.

When we got them back with our residence permits they had been stapled and written on across various pages. Years later, in the UK, we were told the passports had been tampered with and were illegal documents needing immediate replacement.

Our first place of residence was a cockroach-infested apartment in Doha that smelled of mould and damp. A box on the kitchen counter had two bottles of Al Rayan water, Lipton's teabags, UHT milk and a bag of sugar.

Paul went to the university on the first day and I sat alone in the apartment and cried. I was twenty-six and I felt like I'd been dropped off the end of the world.

In Qatar, as in most Middle Eastern countries, the weekends were Thursday and Friday. Saturday was Monday, the first day of the week. The number five looked like a zero and zero was a dot. A backwards three was a four. A backwards seven was a six. The landline phone in our apartment only sported the unfamiliar numbers below that I had to quickly learn to decode.

| ٠ | ١ | ٢ | ٣ | ٤ | ٥ | ٦ | ٧ | ٨ | ٩ |
|---|---|---|---|---|---|---|---|---|---|
| 0 | 1 | 2 | 3 | 4 | 5 | 6 | 7 | 8 | 9 |

Day 1, rule 1: the biggest car on the road always had right of way.

The social hierarchy became obvious quickly. Gulf Arabs were the upper class. Below them the Europeans, then Arabs, then those from South and East Asian countries. All women, however, were at the bottom, as in, if there was any dispute about anything with a man, you would, as a woman, be wrong.

The first afternoon when Paul came home from the university, delivered back safely by the university representatives, the head of department called. I could hear his voice loud on the phone.

'Your wife,' said the head of department. 'Can she teach?'

'Sure,' said Paul.

'Good. Can she be the language lab coordinator and teach phonetics and phonology?'

'Sure,' said Paul.

'Good,' said the head of department. 'She can start on Saturday.'

Our later conversation went something like this:

'I'm sorry,' Paul said. 'I didn't exactly feel I was being asked. But it's great. You'll have a job too now.'

'You could have at least said we would talk about it.'

'I didn't feel there was any way you could refuse.'

'What the fuck is that subject anyway?'

'No idea,' he said. 'I'll get the textbook for you tomorrow.'

*

In August, temperatures and humidity were at their maximum. The air was heavy, wet. It burned my lungs as I inhaled. Heat shimmered in mirages as I walked across acres of expansive sandstone paving towards the entrance on the women's side of the university. Ahead of me, huge concrete sentinels stood

13

against the dusty sky. The buildings were made of blocks also the colour of desert sand, each block probably three cubic metres in size. The structure was as unfamiliar as anything I might have encountered on another planet. Each section of the building was an octagonal construct. Classrooms were octagonal. Atop the buildings were giant concrete block cooling towers, their vertical vents or round lattice vents looking like alien eyes watching. The austerity of the external environment was mirrored by the vacuous and empty courtyards I entered. There were women, of course. Many of them covered. There were no notices, though, no signs of activity, nothing to show the newcomer that she had entered a university. The sections I walked through centred around the open-air cooling towers. From the outside the towers stood out like one-eyed chimney sentinels, but from the inside they hovered overhead, sucking in wind so that cool air descended through the vents and sank into the buildings, while hot air rose and seeped out.

I was lost, that first day. I wandered through a maze of octagons, past the non-sequentially numbered classrooms, past women who were for the most part, silhouettes. I knew I looked bewildered. I felt the draughts beneath the towers as the gaps high above caught and drank in the wind and sent it downward. It drafted through corridors and into a central gathering area — still hot, but less oppressive than how it felt outside and I stopped and asked a young woman to please point me to Room 263, which wasn't anywhere to be seen near Room 264. Kindly, she offered to walk me there. I followed her sweeping black form. I felt the presence of emptiness, despite the chatter of women in groups in a language with sounds I couldn't comprehend or begin to decode.

*

My university teaching career began that Saturday in the language lab at the university, on the women's side. Room 263, an octagonal language lab.

The thirty young women who faced me represented, to my unaccustomed Western view, different degrees of vanishing. Some women were dressed in jeans with long-sleeved shirts or tunics. Some wore headscarves. About a third of the class wore abayas that cloaked everything but their faces. And at least two women were completely covered – so that from time to time I might catch a glimmer of an eye behind the fine mesh of their face coverings.

\*

I introduced the course. Welcome to Phonetics and Phonology. A guide to English pronunciation. Our textbook is called *Ship or Sheep*. Of course, I would diverge from the prescribed text into conversation, discussion and other immersive ways of exploring the necessary language acquisition skills. But this was only day one, and I was speaking into an alien environment where I had no idea what impact any of my words might be having.

\*

'Here's the phonetic alphabet,' I said, to my first of five groups. Somewhere in the day, in the back row, on the right, sat a fresh-faced student with lively eyes who introduced herself as Shaimaa Khalil. She had a liltingly beautiful somewhat-American accent. What was she doing in this pronunciation course? 'Where did you learn English?' I asked. 'It's perfect!'

'We lived in Miami,' you said. 'My mum was doing her PhD at Miami University and we lived there for a short while. My sister and I went to school there when we were kids.'

I felt a rush of gratitude. I thought that maybe in this foreign place, I had found an ally. I didn't know that the desert was as foreign to you as it was to me. You just stood out – a small sliver of radiance in the confusion.

I didn't know, too, that you would become at first, my Rosetta Stone, the key to unlocking the alien world that I had just entered, and later, part of my soul.

# 5.

# SHAIMAA

What a horrible introduction to a place! I can picture you and Paul in that dinky (old) airport surrounded by people you don't understand, not knowing anyone, embarking on a life that seemed so foreign and so unwelcoming.

It's so interesting the way you've picked up on the hierarchy. I'd say there's more than one. Nationality is the big divider; then there's age, gender, occupation, religion, sect.

Work your way up from there all the way to Gulf Arab men with expensive cars and overpriced dishdashas.

This wasn't just in Qatar. I had seen class tensions before – but maybe not as up close. In Egypt, for example. City dwellers especially from Cairo and Alexandria would look down upon those from rural areas regardless of their financial status. I know you're African, but I always thought Westerners – white folk – were right up there in that hierarchy. That's why what happened to you in the airport is extra shocking to me – not that it was okay to happen to anyone else. But I can see them being dismissive of South Asian workers, or of other Arabs like us, but not of white people!

The hierarchy is as disturbing as it is fascinating. One of the things I'm most grateful for is being exposed to so many nationalities from the region. That never happened back home. Egypt is huge. Not just in its geography and physical space, but its culture and spirit. I know everyone says that about their home-country but there's something about Egypt that is all-consuming.

It's right at the heart of the Middle East and, for all intents and purposes, it *is* the heart of the Middle East. It's an Arab country, an African country and a Mediterranean country, one of the oldest civilisations in the world. My grandma's house is older than some cities in the USA. Egypt is the centre of the film and entertainment industry – it's also home to some of the oldest universities in the region. As a child, even when I lived in the USA, I always thought Egypt was the centre of the world.

In the parts of my mind that yearn for certain memories, it still is.

But while it's geographically diverse, Egypt is oppressively homogenous, socially. Growing up, I never came across anyone who was very different from me. Mind you, I was in a Coptic school before we moved to Miami so, in a way, I was lucky to have had Christian friends in school. As a child, it didn't even cross my mind that they were a minority. They were my friends and schoolmates.

*

Living in Qatar, surreal as it was, allowed me to get to know the Middle East better. Gaza, Damascus, Beirut, Algiers, Amman, Baghdad … they weren't abstract notions of cities anymore. I made friends from these places; they became real. And the more real they became, the less Egypt felt like the centre of the world, which was (and still is) quite destabilising for me. By the time I left Doha, I could tell the difference between a Palestinian, Lebanese and Syrian accent. I could easily make out Iraqis from the way they spoke. I could tell from the thobes where in the Gulf a group of men were from. The Qataris, Omanis and the Emiratis are the easiest to spot. It also made me appreciate the South Asian community. It meant that years later when I went to live in Pakistan, it actually wasn't at all foreign. I would've never had that in Egypt. For that experience alone, I'll forever be grateful that I lived in Qatar.

*

But it wasn't without its painful realisations: apart from our mum's salary and medical benefits we had very few rights; the fact that when officials from both countries had a fight it meant that citizens of this country could be let go.

In 1997, a year or so after we moved to Doha, I remember my mother watching the news, which was odd – she doesn't watch TV. She gets her news from newspapers and radio. It was a press conference. The Qatari foreign minister at the time, one of the most powerful men in the country after the Emir (the ruler), was speaking about Egypt. I can't remember what he said but I could make out it wasn't good. He was criticising the Egyptian government in a diplomatic row. He was also making the point that Qatar, while smaller than some neighbourhoods in Cairo (a point Egyptians always make when there are tensions between the two nations), was quite powerful and effective in the area. That was true. Qatar was finding its stride in the Middle East. It was one of the richest nations, per capita, in the area. It seemed that this generation of rulers wanted to make their mark domestically and internationally. They wanted to be the small country with the big presence and one of their biggest projects was Al Jazeera – the newly launched channel and a revolution in the Arabic-speaking news scene at the time – which was funded by the Qatari government.

I wasn't aware of the details at the time. All I knew was that tension was high between my home and host countries and it was bad enough for my mother to follow it live and be worried about it afterwards. It was also bad enough that Egyptian students, including myself, were picked on at university the next day. 'Ooooh you're in trouble!' one girl said to me. She wasn't Qatari. 'Are you going to get kicked out of here?' someone asked. 'Maybe, they're going to fire all Egyptians,' another replied. My heart sank. Were they going to fire my mother? But we just got here! I thought. What did she do? What could she have done? These girls are saying 'all Egyptians'. What did 'all Egyptians' in Qatar do to deserve to be kicked out? I didn't dare ask Mum. I didn't want to worry her. Especially when I overheard her saying, 'We all found it very difficult to sleep after this press conference. It was a tough night,' to a friend. I'd never heard her speak like this. I could always feel her anxiety – I absorbed it like a sponge. But her words pierced right through me.

I think this was the first time I understood what it meant to be an expat in the Gulf. How fragile this life of ease and relative privilege could be. And that what this life made up for in financial reward it took away in stability and security.

I learned later that Egypt had boycotted the MENA conference hosted by Qatar and that the Qatari government was quite indignant at the way Egypt had dealt with the matter. Saudi intervened in the end but that didn't save the jobs of hundreds of Egyptians who were laid off only a few weeks after the mediation. It also didn't help workers who were denied visas in the aftermath. It was my first brush with how the political got very personal. And how tussles between the rich and the powerful directly affected those just trying to get by. Those people had moved to this country in the hope of making their lives better only for them to be told they're no longer wanted because officials they'd never met, for reasons they didn't understand, were stuck in a powerplay. It didn't matter what your position was – street cleaner, doctor, teacher, accountant, university professor – if you weren't a Qatari national (and it is the case in pretty much all Gulf countries), you were disposable. You could be let go and replaced immediately.

This perpetual temporariness coloured everything. The ongoing joke was that all Egyptians get their bags ready every year until they're told to stay another one. The more we stayed in Doha, got used to the comfort and the circle of friends we made, and the more we got settled at university, the scarier the threat of going back to Egypt became with each passing day.

For all of its limitations, there was something liberating about being in Doha. There, I was a stranger and that allowed me to make and occupy my own bubble. It was a place where I could escape the tyranny of familiarity my home country imposed on me. The childhood, the memories, the stifling spoken and unspoken rules of society and extended family. Though it did present its own challenges, of course.

My life in Qatar was full of contradictions, even though I wasn't fully aware of it at the time. From the get-go, however, it struck me as this very odd mix of aridness and modernity. The fast cars, the shops, the desert, the high-walled houses. The nearly empty streets most of the time. A huge departure from the overcrowded noisy Egyptian streets.

In the mid-nineties when we moved there, Doha didn't have much going for it. It was a small capital city of a small Gulf country. It had one shopping centre called 'The Centre'. A few years later there was the grand opening of its first mall called 'The Mall'. The skyline had one distinct building, the pyramid-shaped Sheraton. It's quite remarkable how in just a few years this skyline would change. More high-rise buildings. Bigger malls. The education city complex with different university campuses.

I loved the promenade – the famous Corniche. A beautiful walkway by the gulf water. A walkway I never used as much as I wanted to. Either because the weather was too hot and humid or because there was no one to walk with me. I don't remember ever attempting to walk alone.

I remember Arab expat families gathering there on Friday nights in autumn and winter. It was one of very few outdoor outings available. I never saw Qatari families out by the Corniche at least not in the early days of us being there. Qatari men, yes. Many of them. But no women.

Women's outings were mainly limited to the shops or other women's homes. For those who were employed, their segregated workplaces and Qatar University, a realm of confined intrigue all on its own. The university was a mix of a girls' school and social club atmosphere with a lot of repressed energy.

Shopping in Doha was another incongruously glorious experience. Despite the general emptiness of the city, the stores were stacked. You could find all the mid-nineties trends and brands: clothes, shoes, perfumes, accessories ... things my sister and I only saw in magazines back home in Alexandria. The American magazines that we had to save up to buy were right there in the shops in Doha.

Even the supermarkets were overwhelming. All those chocolates our cousins who lived in Saudi would come back to Egypt with during the summer holidays ... we could have them whenever we wanted. The variety compared to Egypt was jaw dropping. It was my and my sister's closest proximity to high octane consumerism. That was the main sport in the Gulf. Buying things. Qatar was no exception. That's what most women in Doha did as a pastime.

And there was no place where this was more on display than the women's building at Qatar University.

I soon realised that this was one of the very few places women got to show off their latest purchases.

One of my most enduring memories of this segregated labyrinth of a place that is Qatar University was that wave of colour unfolding the further the women got from the main gate.

I'd see them walk in, all looking the same in their black abayas, covered from head to toe, and as soon as they cross the threshold into the women's campus it all changed.

'The QU Catwalk!' I'd say to myself as I rushed to my classes, wondering how long it took those women to organise their outfits and how in the world some got their eyeshadow to match the shade of their blouse.

You would hear the clack of high heels in a sea of brands: Louis Vuitton, Gucci, Prada – Calvin Klein and Ralph Lauren for the more casual looks – all making their way to different classrooms for the first lecture of the day.

When I first enrolled at Qatar University, my mother, who was a professor there, told me about a dress code.

'A uniform? At university, Mummy?'

'A dress code. These are the rules here,' she said.

These were the rules and I had to abide by them. Not just because I'd be penalised but also because the way I behaved reflected directly on my mother.

I had two long skirts made, which I struggled to walk in – one black, one navy blue – and bought two long-sleeved shirts. That was my uniform. No brands. No makeup.

And while most of the women stuck to the so-called dress code, it was obvious how they got around the rules. In all my life I'd never seen so many skin-tight long skirts, some ill-fitted; I worried what would happen if these girls sat down. And shirts so snug, buttons were at risk of flying off in every direction. On paper though … they were 'as per the dress code'. Some women let their hair show, while others had coloured headscarves under their black headscarves. There were also those who dressed conservatively and so beautifully. I remember marvelling at how some girls moved so gracefully in their abbayas and jilbabs. How the colour of their hijabs was perfectly coordinated with the pattern on their abbayas or skirts. My favourites were the sporty ones – who still stuck to the dress code but with long-sleeved T-shirts, long skirts and Air Jordans. Every day was a new lesson in fashion. Not that I learned anything!

Another scene etched in my memory was that of the fleeting moments when women crossed paths with male professors in the corridors. Not wishing to be seen, some women would use their books and folders to cover their faces, all with the tight skirts and shirts still in full view – I never got the point of that, and I could only imagine how awkward it was for the male professors.

It was such a melange of fashion and tastes. From the tomboys to the bling fashionistas. All within 'the dress code'.

It was a lot to navigate and of course it was easy to falter with so many rules. I remember early on being pulled aside and given a written warning because my sleeves were not long. I was petrified that this would affect my mother's reputation and job if they worked out that I was her daughter.

Despite the bumpy start, once I got through the first year of deciphering my surroundings and got over any ambitions for a 'real college experience', my time at QU was well spent. For the first time in my education I excelled academically. I was studying something I loved, English.

I gained unexpected skills that were not really useful anywhere else. I got really good at telling the girls apart even when they were fully covered. Just from their eyes and from their voice. I become attuned to the different Arabic dialects. I could tell you if a girl was from Qatar, Bahrain or Saudi. I could also distinguish between Palestinian, Syrian and Jordanian accents and gained a new appreciation for my Egyptian accent, which was the most loved among everyone as it always reminded them of popular films and TV shows.

While it didn't do miracles for my social life, Qatar University allowed me a decent education with close proximity to great teachers. Ultimately, it was where I met you. And in that sense it was life-changing.

The thing I appreciate the most about my Doha experience is that it gave me my first taste of being an outsider – which I now realise is my perpetual status.

The starkest contradiction of all was that living in Doha tested my idea of home. I lived there for ten years before I moved to London. My mother and sister, more than twenty. For many Arab expat families, plans to move to the Gulf start as temporary attempts to make a better living and then move back to the homeland – but end up lasting decades because of the opportunities and the lifestyle.

Despite the difficulty getting used to life there as young teenagers, my sister and I made beautiful memories and friendships through the years. Some, like ours, that have endured through time. We both got our degrees from Qatar University. We got our first jobs in Doha. Met our husbands there. I left for the UK and my sister started a family in Doha. Two of her children went to school there. When I went back for family visits it was split between Egypt and Qatar. They both felt like home and in their own ways they both didn't.

Our roots are in Egypt, in Alexandria no doubt. But our lives had branched out and neither I nor my sister felt like we had a place there anymore.

Our youth and early adulthood were shaped in Qatar. My sister was bringing up her children there. It never crossed my mind the difficulty of raising a child and explaining why the place where they were born, where they went to school and where their parents lived and worked was not home in the true sense. I remember visiting Doha once and having dinner with my sister and her kids. I'm not sure what the actual conversation was. But I do remember my nephew referring to Qatar as 'our country'. My sister and her husband fell silent, smiled, and then she said, 'Habibi (my love), Qatar is technically not our country but it's our home "for now". Egypt is officially our country, although we don't live there.' He looked a bit confused but then carried on fiddling with his food.

For me – working for QBS – Qatar's local English radio station, was more than just a job. It started my career and fuelled my love for music (hip-hop mainly!) and broadcasting. This is where I knew what it was like to have a relationship with the microphone. This is where I learned about the power of the voice. That little studio in the Radio and TV building in Doha was the seed of all my journalistic ambitions. That and pretending to be a presenter when I was a kid staring at the wall like it was a camera! QBS is also where I met the man I love. My husband, Ahmed, who worked as a producer in the radio newsroom. In many ways, I am where I am now because of that life in Doha.

And yet for all it offered, it never really felt like home. It always felt like our whole existence was dependent on a job. That the lives my sister and I built were a contract-renewal or contract-termination away from being upended.

'Like many expats, you would have a great lifestyle and a beautiful house to enjoy. But not a home to retire in,' my sister, Shaza, said. 'It's like I was living in a beautiful hotel for twenty-three years. Although I moved out, I feel very connected to the fabulous memories and wonderful friends I made there,' she said.

It's amazing how permanent a 'temporary' arrangement can become. As hard as it was to set roots in Doha, I think it was ideal for my runaway spirit. My 'be-ready-to-leave-at-any-moment' self was born there and it's become the core of the job that I do and love now.

# 6.

# SHELLEY

The subtleties of the social hierarchies eluded me. I didn't know where everyone fitted in, but I learned fast that women couldn't do anything without men, regardless of ethnicity. Doha was such a contradiction: being in the Middle East rescued us from poverty. It gave us status. We had jobs, an income, positions teaching at university. In so many ways I could not believe my luck. Growing up in South Africa, violence was a part of everyday life. Bearing witness to crimes happened all too often. I could not cope with what I saw, what I heard, what I feared. I was desperate to leave. I knew a South African passport would be prohibitive. Marrying Paul was as desperate as it was romantic. Because he was born in England, and was brought to Africa when he was three weeks old, he had a British passport. That small slice of First World documentation was enough. When we got married, I acquired a free pass into the coveted 'West'. Our marriage was my runaway ticket. It allowed us to be together – to leave Africa and land in England legitimately. I felt like I'd been given a life raft. I felt certain that if I stayed in South Africa it would have devoured me.

In London, me on a temporary spousal visa attached to Paul, Paul applying for hundreds of jobs everywhere, he received the offer from Qatar University.

We felt saved. Rescued. We did the most indulgent thing we could think of: we ran all the way through South Norwood, through Crystal Palace, to a patisserie on a High Street. We each bought a full, crusty, toasted brie, basil and tomato baguette – the most expensive item on the menu. It was the end of living in poverty. Having white-enough skin had allowed me to sneak into England without being detected. I felt like a Third World child, but this skin, this accent, enabled me to blend in. It was easy to start sounding British. I hid my fear that the bottom line was that if anything went wrong, I would be back in South Africa.

*

In Doha I had my first salary come into my account. It was one-third of Paul's even though I worked twice the hours. I had to teach on the men's side of the university too. And the young men, some Qatari, some from Yemen, some from Jordan, some from Palestine – they were polite. But they told me outright on my second day: 'We do not like to be taught by a woman, Mrs Shelley.'

'Oh,' I said. 'Why's that?'

'Because,' said Jassim. 'What can a woman know?'

At first I thought it was funny. Then Mohammed said, 'Why does your husband allow you to teach?'

I laughed. 'Well, he doesn't allow me. He has no say in what I do or don't do. I teach because I want to teach.'

'But that is not your job,' said Mohammed. 'You should be at home. You should stay home and have children.'

'I like teaching,' I said. 'And I'm sorry you're not happy with having a woman teach you – but that's the way of the world outside of Qatar, and that's how it's going to be while I'm here. I've been hired to teach you. You'll have to get used to it.'

They accepted, grudgingly, their fate.

Women worked in Qatar, but in the crevices and shadows of a man's world. It felt like a transgression, just going out on any given day. I imagine it would be like walking naked out of your house in Australia, getting in your car, going to work, and walking down the footpaths and up office stairs without any clothes on. People would stare. You'd feel vulnerable, absurd. Even teaching at the university, I felt my own presence vibrating at a high frequency in a way I'd never experienced before. I was stared at, by men, by women, everywhere I went. I had an unbearable desire to cover myself up – to dive beneath an abaya and vanish. Expat women had jobs – in banks, at the university, in teaching. Westerners, in particular, could teach on both sides of the university. So there were men teaching on the women's side of the campus. When I walked across the courtyard with Paul on the women's side, women held their books and bags in front of their faces to avoid being gazed on by him. And there were several expat women teaching on the men's side. I did not see any of my female Qatari colleagues ever teach on the men's side. Still, I felt a new empowerment for the first time in my life. Money does that to a person.

*

One day, after a week or two of being in Doha, Paul and I, both teaching on the women's side that day, went out into the heat and sat on a bench. We were sharing a sandwich. Through the windows, young women were peering at us, banging on the glass. 'Excuse me! Excuse me!' someone called. Some of the women came outside, but then went in again. They giggled. They shouted at one another. They didn't approach us. We didn't know what was going on. But something was amiss. I wanted to ask someone what we'd done wrong. There was no one at that moment whom I could turn to for advice.

The young women in my language lab class were curious about my background.

'I came from London,' I said. 'But I was born in South Africa.'

They liked that I came from London.

'Mrs. Shelley, how old are you?'

'Twenty-seven.'

Some of them laughed. 'Nayrouz is as old as you!'

Nayrouz sat in the front row. She was nine months pregnant.

'Were you always a teacher?' Manal asked.

I didn't want to tell them that this was my first ever teaching position.

'I've done other things. I'm a writer. I write books for Macmillan in the UK.'

After the class, you stayed.

'So, what do you write?' you asked.

'Different things. A lot of children's books, novels. Poetry.'

'Cool. Can I read one of your books?'

'Really?'

'Yeah!'

'Okay, but on condition that if you get bored, you don't read it!'

You laughed. I was touched that you were interested in actually reading any of my books.

'At some point,' I said. 'Can I ask you a question about the culture here that you might be able to answer for me?'

'Sure,' you said. 'Anytime.'

'Not here, not now. But sometime. Thanks. I'm trying to figure stuff out here. I don't want to offend anyone but I may have already done this.'

You smiled. 'Sure.'

I asked you about your family.

'My dad's in Egypt. I'm here with my mum and sister.'

Egypt. I know we talked more, and that I thought you were lovely. Mature. Open. You were from a land I'd dreamt about all through my teens. I love how you describe Egypt – that it has a heart. That it's all-consuming – a confluence of East and West and Middle East – but also Africa. When I was eighteen and nineteen, I lived in a mythical Egypt in my head. The fact that Egypt was in Africa made me feel like I was born on a valuable continent with ancient traditions that were full of mystery and magic. I went through a two- or three-year phase of painting and drawing giant pictures of cobras and dung beetles and pyramids and I did several portraits of Tutankhamun and used gold-leaf paint. So I was painting pharaohs and you were nine then.

I try to imagine you, being a nine- or ten-year-old girl in the land of Tutankhamun – in this place where cultures and perspectives collided.

After that conversation, I knew I could ask you about how and why the eating-outside-incident was so obviously a transgression of some kind.

A week later, you said, 'I've read your book. I want to talk to you about it.'

That, I believe, is when I gave you my phone number.

You called.

I don't recall the exact conversation, but it ended with me inviting you to come and have a cup of tea at our apartment.

Unlike the other women students, you weren't ferried around by a driver. You had a car. You drove to visit us.

You arrived on a hot Friday afternoon. You knocked on the glass door of our air-conditioned apartment and I saw your shadow, and ran to let you in.

You entered the corridor on a gust of warm air; you reminded me of myself ten years earlier, hopeful, idealistic. You looked like any Western teenager in your jeans and T-shirt. And you were comfortable straight away. While I made tea, you went into the lounge and chatted with Paul.

We sat down on the couch together and I handed you a cup of tea. 'So here's the question. The other day, Paul and I sat down to eat on a bench in the courtyard on the women's side. There was a lot of frenzied action and giggling and shouting. The girls everywhere were going crazy. Did we do something wrong?'

You nodded and smiled. 'It's kind of like if you guys were in London and you went to work naked and then started making out naked and in public. It's just not done. These are things – being together, eating food together, that have to stay out of the public eye.'

My first lesson: men and women sitting together casually out in the open was not allowed.

Eating in public: very frowned upon.

A man and a woman sitting together *and* eating in public: a cultural transgression.

In this segregated society, perhaps we should have known.

*

From then on, there were no more shared sandwiches on the bench. Or anywhere on campus.

The university campus was divided down the middle into the men's and women's side. I had to go through a checkpoint with a guard to teach the men. The two sides of the university were like night and day. I don't know if you knew this, but the men's side had an Olympic-sized swimming pool, where no one as far as I saw, ever swam, despite outside temperatures of over fifty degrees Celsius sometimes. They had a library, vast corridors and empty rooms that were newer and cleaner than any classrooms on the women's side. Also, there were hardly any men on that side, because the local Qatari men (some of whom belonged to the royal family) were sent overseas to study, to London and New York and San Francisco. I had a class of seven men, and five classes of thirty women to teach. On the women's side I smiled and laughed and hugged my students. On the men's side I had to cast my eyes down if any man walked past. I felt like I was learning an alien language. On several occasions when I drove home from the university on my own, young men tried to drive me off the road into the desert. I learned to drive our two-door Hyundai Scoupe like a racing driver. I did not know if these were the same men I taught, behaving like hooligans. I didn't know what would happen if they did manage to ride me into the desert. I usually rode with Paul because nothing like that ever happened when I was with him. So, in this highly segregated society, where Pizza Hut and McDonald's had a men's entrance, and a family entrance for women and children, where banks were segregated, where I learned that women never met men except when this was arranged, or chaperoned, you drove around in your own little car, navigating Doha as a young woman.

# 7.

# SHAIMAA

I remember talking to you in class felt as easy and natural as talking to a long-time friend or a family member. You had none of that haughtiness many professors put on to maintain their authority. You gave me your autobiographical novel *Freefalling*.

'I can't believe all of this happened to you!' I said after I finished it.

'Which part?' You smiled.

'Did someone really hit you in the face with a satchel?' I said, not giving you much chance to answer. 'Was it really that bad? Were you scared for your life all the time? Did people you knew die?'

I had so many questions about South Africa, this part of my continent I had no idea about. Nelson Mandela was a symbol of freedom and resistance. That's all I knew.

You were so lovely and patient explaining the hell that was apartheid and the violence that ensued during and even after it ended.

You gave me another one of your books. A short novel. And I remember marvelling at the fact that I knew this 'real-life' author – someone who had lived in and seen the world. A world I so wanted to see and experience.

I also knew that the way to that was financial independence. I needed a job. One of my good friends at uni had got a summer job as a trainee at a bank. It was one of the few jobs available to women at the time. Jobs were available in banks, schools, and women's sections in different public sector offices and government departments. I didn't see myself in any of those jobs while at university.

I loved music and the local English radio station QBS was the go-to place for the Top 40 countdown. I'd tried to call their main number and speak to someone about an internship but got nowhere. Until I found out that one of the older students at the English department at QU, a fellow Egyptian, was one of the very few women who worked at the station. She generously agreed to introduce me to the station manager but whether or not they took me on was up to them of course.

I'll always be grateful to her for that first push and will always remember my first ever time in a radio studio. Those padded, soundproof walls. The radio desk and the faders! I know it's a major cliché but this was the only 'love at first sight' moment I had. It started as a summer job filling in for expat continuity presenters when they were on vacation. Continuity presenters came on between programs to tell listeners what was coming up in the next few hours. There was a real art to making something mundane sound interesting and not repeating yourself all the time. I ended up working in the station as a radio DJ for seven years. It's where I fell in love with broadcasting. And where I got to play music and get paid for it!

That first salary. I remember it so well. It was from my first ever summer job at QBS radio. It couldn't have been more than 1500 Riyals a month – about 580 AUD – in the late nineties. Not a huge amount, but my GOD it felt so good.

I knew then I wanted to feel that way all the time if I could. I'm not sure what felt more liberating at the time – getting my first salary, or finally being able to drive and use my mum's car in Doha.

I'd spent the summer of '98 driving my dad's old car in Alexandria. This was one of the best summers I remember. Ironically, it turned out to be the last summer I'd ever spend with my dad. Not that I spent enough time with him. He was mostly in the hospital and I was mostly avoiding him. We had a tense relationship. I also hated seeing him as ill as he was.

I learned later that he took taxis to his dialysis sessions so that I could go to the beach with my friends in his car.

It's funny because I hate driving. I realised that only when I knew I had the choice, and also when I later moved to London and had the option of safe, (mostly) dependable public transport. All I needed was something to get me from A to B – without being sexually harassed. In Egypt that was not guaranteed with public transport and in Doha, well, there was no public transport.

I might go back to driving. I'm not sure. There are parts of it I miss, the classic stuff – listening to one of my favourite songs and driving in peace.

I don't miss being followed around on the road by men in Doha and having them park right outside our building. Some actually would get out of the car to talk to me and my sister. Over time I think we became very good at driving around and losing them. Some got bored, others thought it was a game. It was a constant worry. Which is why, for example, we wouldn't laugh or smile too much in the car, especially at a red light or in a traffic jam. We'd definitely avoid catching anyone's eye in these situations because all of this could be seen as an 'invitation' to be followed and harassed.

My God, to think of you having to deal with *all* this nonsense so soon after you arrived. What a shock that must have been!

I can't believe they tried to push you off the road. I can only imagine what that must've felt like for you when all you did was get in a car to get back home.

My sister Shaza has this interesting theory about road harassment, and it goes back to the hierarchy too. The year she and her family were getting ready to leave Doha and move to Canada, Shaza and her husband sold their two luxury cars and bought a smaller one off one of Mohamed's friends. Shaza told me this was her worst year on the road.

She was a woman driving a cheap car.

She said that expensive or luxury cars weren't just about comfort and status, they were also a message to those on the road that the person in that car was not to be messed with. I'm not sure how accurate this theory is, but I always drove cheap cars and I was regularly messed with!

Her theory has also confirmed another struggle (among many) for me living in the Middle East: this pathological concern with looks and status, whether it was social or religious. What you put on your back (or your head) had consequences – much more for women than men of course. I know it's true all over the world, but I think it goes to a whole new level in conservative societies … I've always wondered why those who insisted on women covering themselves were so obsessed with what women wore, where they went and with whom.

One of the things I valued most about living in London was that I could go out in my pyjamas and no one would care. The irony of course is that with my headscarf I developed a different kind of status. 'The-Muslim-Girl-in-the-West-Representing' status. In the Middle East it was easy to blend in with a headscarf. In the 'Post-9/11 West', a time when Islam was in focus (for all the wrong reasons), wearing a hijab was a statement whether I liked it or not.

I swayed into different modes. The 'I'm going to show the world that Muslim women can make it here too' mode. The 'It's just a headscarf, I don't want to represent anything or anyone' mode. The 'I'm not an interpreter or a spokesperson for Islam mode'. None of them worked; all of them were exhausting. Whether it was at home in Egypt, in Qatar or in the UK – I spent my life trying to fit in and it's always hard work.

I dare generalise that women in the Middle East and in conservative societies as a whole develop a very subtle art of leading double lives. We get really good, really fast at bending the rules and living within their crevices. We also get crafty at living with contradictions.

When you live in a society where some of the men who tell you to cover yourself and stay out of the way, or who lecture you about chastity, are the same ones who sexually harass and abuse you, you *have* to learn to accept hypocrisy as a life companion.

Women grow up watching their fathers, brothers and male cousins do the exact things they're being told they cannot do only by virtue of their gender.

To this day I'll never forget how heartbroken I was when I realised I could no longer play in the street but boys could because well … they were boys! Scale that up to every aspect of life. One of the reasons I started to smoke at one point (even though I hate the taste of cigarettes) was that I was told that if a boy is seen with a cigarette, it was part of him wanting to be a man, but if a girl is seen with one, she brings her family shame.

It was a small act of rebellion. Because why would this disgusting tube of tobacco and tar bring shame on my family just because it was me, a woman, smoking it? I was fascinated by stories other girls would share – whether in Doha or back home in Alexandria – about their boyfriends. Meeting them, spending time, explaining gifts and flowers to their parents. How! I would think. The stress!

So many of us existed in this double reality. We manipulated the rules and bent them. We enjoyed the buzz of our brush with danger. Cigarettes, shorter sleeves and skirts. Hushed phone calls with crushes we wouldn't dare be seen with in public. Hands held briefly and stolen kisses – secret teenage triumphs. The consequences of being found out were real. We hoped that we wouldn't get caught and if one of us did, the rest of us would pray silently for their safety and their families' and society's mercy.

I know I don't represent all women of course, and that restrictions will vary, but I can confidently bet that a version of this double existence is true for many women in conservative societies.

Some women embrace the rules and restrictions fully and pass it on to the next generation. Others spend their life fighting. And then there are those like me, who pour every inch of their being into trying to escape and looking for a way and a place to be themselves if they're lucky enough to know who that is.

Those who do escape have to endure the bad joke of realising that these social restrictions and double standards have been etched into our DNA wherever we go, and that when we return to our respective homes, we go back to navigating them.

My hat is always off to my single friends in these societies who have to prove every day that they are whole, complete human beings. And to mothers who want to bring up their boys and girls equally in every sense.

Mind you here I am … married. And on the face of it at least, I have stopped fighting the Big Bad Patriarch or at least learned to live at a safe distance. I'm not sure if I'm just tired or if I've never actually dared to fight in the first place. I honestly don't know. I can't tell you for sure that I know who I am. All I know is that I need to be responsible for my own existence and not ask for permission, and that is still a struggle.

# 8.

# SHELLEY

I'm haunted by the image of your dad going to dialysis by taxi in Egypt so you could have his car.

I'm haunted by the arrest of my own dad in the early 1990s by a white Afrikaans policeman on the evening before he was to emigrate to Canada with my stepmum and their two young children. He had spent his working life being overly generous in South Africa to poor people. As a pharmacist, he gave away medicines and supplies to poor black people who needed it. He was, as the Jewish people said, a 'mensch'. A man with a big, generous heart. He knew the suffering of the poor, the oppressed. The Holocaust was in his DNA. Of course, he went bankrupt.

*

The white Afrikaans policeman who arrested him in front of my little sister said, 'Now we will teach you fucking Jews a lesson.' My dad had grown up on a farm. His dad spoke to him in English and Afrikaans. He spoke Afrikaans without an accent. My dad was a South African Jew who spoke and

40

wrote fluent Afrikaans and who dispensed medicine and help to anyone who needed it. Jews were viewed as the 'blacks of Europe'. They have a complex place in South African history, finding themselves at the receiving end of racism and later sometimes aligning themselves with the racists perhaps to avoid the harsh discriminatory practices of a violent, oppressive government.

My dad's crime was that he owed money, because he could not look on suffering without offering help whenever and wherever it was needed.

Even though he was released soon after, and even though his criminal case was quickly assigned as a civil case, he lost his Canadian residence and we, who had applied with him to emigrate to Canada, all lost residence with him.

My dad spent the rest of his life in South Africa. During that time he was held up at gunpoint. Tied up with his wife in their living room and threatened with his life. He was hijacked. Robbed. He had never hurt anyone or wished anyone harm. He was the kindest of men.

No one in Doha knew I was Jewish.

Jews and Muslims. According to the world, we're at war.

*

One day, shortly after your first visit to our apartment in your mum's car, I was teaching my small class of seven men – three from Qatar, one from Jordan, two from Palestine and one from Syria.

The men knew that Paul was my husband. It was the one thing that gave me a shred of immunity against potential hostility. Out of respect to him, they would not risk upsetting his wife. They tolerated me, though they made it clear that women's autonomy to work or have agency was not a well-tolerated idea.

'We are doing *Gatsby* with Dr Paul. I don't like that book at all. All that it shows about the West – it's what we think. It is decadent and evil.'

'Oh,' I said. 'Tell me more about that.'

'They are always drinking in the book. Alcohol is the great evil and everyone is eventually punished and we should not feel sorry for these characters. The women are loose. There is no honour. And that's why Gatsby has to die. And Daisy,' Mahmoud said. 'It's a good moral.'

'Okay,' I said. 'That's an interesting interpretation.'

'It confirms what I already feel. I hate the West,' Bassel said.

'What do you hate about it?' I asked. It was as if I hadn't figured out where I was and could not decode the code; I wasn't yet accustomed to the layers of appearance vs reality, of what you do and say as opposed to what it looks like you do and say. How appearance was everything, and keeping face was everything, regardless of the reality.

'Look,' he said, lifting his T-shirt for everyone to see. His abdomen was criss-crossed with deep scars. 'I was thirteen living in Palestine. My mother was sick and I had to go and run to find her medicine. An Israeli soldier chased me, he caught me, and he shot me – here. And I couldn't get medicine for my mother, because I was injured.'

As he told me his story, my heart sank into the pit of my stomach. I felt sick. I wanted to cry for this boy, for the child he was, for the cruelty he'd suffered. I looked at his brown eyes and saw there the eyes of my younger brother, who looked so much like him. For a moment I was with him in his despair, in his hatred of the man who had done this to him, to his family. And then Bassel said, 'that is why, if I see a Jew, I will kill him.'

Silence.

I was so immersed in his anguish, it took me a while to register that I was a Jew.

If he knew, this young man whose story had just broken my heart might want to kill me, not because of who I was, but because of who I would represent.

'I'm so sorry, Bassel. That's terrible,' I said. He dropped his shirt. I went on teaching for a few minutes, but I couldn't finish the lesson.

'Hey guys, you can go early today. You've done a great job.'

It was then that I realised I had to be extra careful about my identity, my history, my story.

*

On my way home, I was driving alone, feeling rattled. A guy in a large four-wheel drive followed me all the way back to the apartment. I parked as close to the lift as I could, got out of my car, and the man rolled down his window and yelled. I ran to the lift, pressed the button, and when it didn't immediately open, I took the stairs, five flights to the top in the fiery hot afternoon. Bursting into the apartment, I said to Paul, 'There's a guy, he followed me home. Please go and look out the window. Is there still a white four-wheel drive parked in the front of the building?'

'Yep. Still there,' Paul said. He stood on the balcony staring down at the man until he left and drove away.

I tried to tell Paul how it felt – to be hunted, harassed like that. To be representative of something. Not myself. Not me.

*

A few days later he came home from work. He rushed in through the front door, slammed it.

'Some guy followed me home,' he said. 'I thought it was a student. He stopped his car next to mine, called me over. When

I went to the window to see what he wanted, he grabbed me, pulled me towards him and tried to kiss me. Can you go out onto the balcony and see if he's still there?'

'Yep, there's a black sports car parked out there. Is that him?'

'That's the guy.'

I watched the car for a while. Eventually the engine roared to life and my husband's stalker blasted out of the car park in a cloud of dust.

'Now I have some idea about how it feels,' he said to me.

Not even he was immune to the behaviour of the Big Bad Patriarch.

\*

Teaching on the men's side of the campus required a particular kind of energy. I was neither wanted, nor respected. I had to steel myself every day. I can't say I wanted to be there. But that was half the job. The other half of the job, on the women's side of the campus gave me life. I loved teaching the women. They worked hard and were dedicated and respectful to a degree I've never experienced before or since. I had never felt so real in my teaching life.

\*

On a day when the heat turned the air to liquid and I stared out of my classroom window through a haze of bent and buckled and melted reality, I finished teaching *Ship or Sheep*, ('Repeat after me and remember that the "p" is a voiceless plosive that you don't have in Arabic and the "b" is voiced, and there's a difference. And I want to hear it.')

They dutifully sat with their headphones on and listened to the recording and repeated the words 'Put it in the pot, Mrs Bloggs.'

After hearing this thirty times, I said, 'Okay, great job. Now, who likes poetry?'

Two thirds of the class raised their hands.

'I want to share some of the poetry I studied and loved at university that I think you may enjoy.' I feared that the archaic language might be a deterrent. Certainly it was light years away from *put it in the pot, Mrs Bloggs*. 'I'll tell you about the Romantics. My favourite is the writer John Keats. He only lived until he was twenty-six and had a heartbreaking relationship with his neighbour, Fanny Brawne, but their love was never consummated – because he was poor, and he got ill and died of tuberculosis. This summer, before I came to Qatar, I went to a special Keats exhibition in London. There I read his words from the 1800s in which he said something like, *I coughed and found a spot of blood upon my pillow. It is arterial blood – this is my death warrant.* I cried – I felt so sad for him. So, this poem is about a knight who falls under the spell of a fairy lady in the woods – and his love for her literally destroys him. You can see how this is based on his own heartbreak. It's got a French title.' The class was silent.

I handed out copies of his ballad *La Belle Dame sans Merci*.

The women bent their heads and took turns reading the poem.

> … She took me to her Elfin grot,
>     And there she wept and sighed full sore,
> And there I shut her wild wild eyes
>     With kisses four.

> And there she lullèd me asleep,
>     And there I dreamed—Ah! woe betide!—
> The latest dream I ever dreamt
>     On the cold hill side.

I saw pale kings and princes too,
 Pale warriors, death-pale were they all;
They cried—'La Belle Dame sans Merci
 Thee hath in thrall!'

Afterwards we discussed it.

'How's the language?' I asked.

'Fine,' Manal said. 'I wish I could marry Keats.'

'Why?'

'He's so passionate. He loves that woman with his whole heart. If there was a poster of him, I'd put him on my wall.'

The others laughed.

'If you married him, he'd have to convert to Islam,' Hend said. 'And how would you meet him anyway?'

'He'd be a time traveller,' Manal said. 'From the past. I'd meet him on the plane returning from a visit that I would get to make with my brothers to London. He'd be blind, so he wouldn't look at my face. We'd spend the journey talking, and by the end, we'd be in love. He would love me and not worry at all anymore about Fanny Brawne. My family would welcome him, and he'd ask to marry me, and convert to Islam. That's how I'd marry Keats.'

I loved her story. I imagined a poetically blind Keats in the twentieth century on a plane meeting young Manal and falling in love with her sweet soul; untainted because he could not look on her, or lust after her, because he couldn't see her – and he would marry her for love.

'What do you find most compelling about the poem?' I asked.

'The fact that the woman has all the power,' Maryam said. 'The knight, or maybe it's Keats himself, needs the woman much more than she needs him.'

The class agreed.

'Your homework is to write a poem in the same vein as Keats – use the ballad form if you like, and bring it next week. Oh, and practise *Ship or Sheep*.'

The room filled with lively chatter – and then, at the window of the classroom, the face of Dr Johara appeared. She peeked in, dark eyes scanning the room, for what, I wondered? Nonetheless, I felt guilty. I waved at her and she vanished. Perhaps she had sensed female energy unleashed.

After class, Manal came to me. Her blue headscarf made her face seem pale. She wrung her bony hands and smiled nervously. 'Mrs Shelley,' she said. 'I wanted to tell you something.'

'Sure, Manal.'

'I'm getting engaged.'

'What, really?'

She looked at me as innocent as a seven-year-old, as pure.

'Is your fiancé anything like Keats?' I asked.

She laughed. Her smile waned. 'No. No. I've talked with him twice. I think he's nice. I don't think he will be very strict. I'd like to invite you to my engagement party.'

'Oh, thank you.'

She didn't think he'd be very strict.

'So it's an arranged marriage?' I asked. She looked at me with condescension, this almost eighteen-year-old.

'Of course.'

'Of course.'

'Our parents know best, Mrs Shelley,' she said as if explaining the facts of life to a young child. 'No one is wise enough to make good choices at our age.'

'You're probably right.'

She looked relieved. 'And you and Mr Paul, was your marriage arranged?'

I shook my head. 'No. We met. We fell in love. We chose each other. Our parents had no say in the matter.'

'Oh,' she said. 'I thought such marriages wouldn't last. I thought that's why the West has such a high rate of divorce.'

'I guess you're right. There is a high rate of divorce. But sometimes it works. I suppose I'm lucky. I married someone who's also my best friend.'

She nodded. 'That's what I hope. That my husband will become my best friend. That maybe one day we will fall in love. That's what my mother says will happen.'

'It sounds good, Manal. Congratulations! I'd be honoured to come and celebrate with you.'

I wondered what these young women's lives were like. So many of them were veiled.

Not you, dear Shaimaa. You were one of the few whose smile I could see every day. When, I wondered, did these women vanish from the public? Was there a time when things changed? When was that for you?

*

I remember you telling me then that your dad had died. And that you and your mum and sister were anxious because his relatives might get custody of you. I felt afraid for you at the time. I couldn't imagine what that meant.

While I was growing up in apartheid South Africa, I bore witness to terrible human rights abuses. The Big Bad Patriarch was always there, but it took me a while to figure out his power. I grew up in the south of the African continent, you grew up in the north – our teen years, experienced ten years apart, our lives inverted mirrors of each other. While you learned how to navigate being a girl of the Middle East, I ran around naked, swam naked in the sea at age one, at four, at twelve, at fifteen and twenty. The Patriarch's hand was present, but more subtle, his cruelty more insidious, as I was growing up.

# 9.

# SHAIMAA

I can't imagine what it was like for your father to be arrested and humiliated like this and for what? For doing good. For helping others that happened to be the oppressed.

Despite trying to educate myself on it over the years, I still can't get my head around what it was like living under apartheid every single day. Where a government and a society consciously and systematically decided to discriminate against its own people in every aspect of life and punish those who helped them.

I know you tried to explain it to me when we were in Doha – what South Africa was like during the time. It's hard to grasp when you haven't lived it.

Many of my Palestinian friends and colleagues, through the years, have tried to explain the human side of the Arab-Israeli conflict. And despite it always being an integral part of the Egyptian psyche, it's one of the most difficult things for me to tackle mentally.

Jerusalem is at the heart of an old, festering wound – a century-old conflict where the bloodshed continues and neither side wins.

The violence in Jerusalem or Gaza (where Hamas – the Islamic Resistance Movement – is in charge) has become regular and almost expected every couple of years. It's become a matter-of-fact conversation in newsrooms across the world about when the next flare up is going be.

*

To me, this isn't just a news story. This has been THE story of my region. It's the story I and hundreds of millions of Arabs grew up with. A story that is so close and so far away all at once. A story that has carved itself into the collective psyche and yet its details and intricacies as the conflict dragged on have eluded many.

Egypt is the most prominent and most strategic broker in this cursed relationship between the Palestinians and Israel; a chief negotiator, a gateway to Gaza, and one of the biggest military powers in the region.

Egypt had its own conflicts with Israel in 1956, 1967 and the war of attrition in the three years that followed. Al Naksa, The Defeat of '67 was a stab in all Egyptian hearts. Thousands of families lost loved ones in that war but the loss of land and the humiliation hurt the most, my parents and grandparents would tell me. Then came the 1973 war, which is known in Egypt as The October War and in the West the Yom Kippur War. Our big victory. Our pride was restored and then political and diplomatic deals were made. Not in the Middle East but in Camp David, the American Presidential resort near Washington DC. The relationship that transpired between Egypt and Israel through the years wasn't so much peace as it was an absence of war. An Israeli embassy was established in Cairo. And an Egyptian one in Tel Aviv. 'But what's in the heart is in the heart,' was the populous sentiment in Egypt. My father was in the army, so was his father. So were the fathers and the grandfathers of so many of my friends.

You'll be hard-pressed to find a household that didn't lose someone in one of those wars or wasn't related to someone who fought in at least one of them.

No two places had been a part of my life without me ever setting foot in them more than Israel and Palestine. And even just by saying that … I know I'm being inaccurate because to this day, a two-state solution remains an elusive notion. This has been going on for so long now that it's a part of our identity and yet I've lost sight of what it's become and how it'll ever be resolved.

Despite it being in my consciousness long before I understood its scale and gravity, no other war baffles me personally and challenges me professionally more than the Arab-Israeli conflict.

*

Then there are the maps …

The maze of borders drawn by pencil and contested by blood.

The geography of the area confuses and flusters me. Geography of course *is* the Arab-Israeli conflict and because of where I work, it's a fraught subject that I've chosen to steer clear from whenever I can. And when I have to cover the story in any way, I feel the need to study and over-prepare for it like it's a test.

Because first and foremost my job requires me to be fair and objective.

I remember the Gaza war in 2008–9. It's a story and a time that still torment me.

It was my first year as a full-time BBC journalist and I wanted to make a point that I was neutral and that I didn't side with people in Gaza just because I was Muslim.

When Gaza was being bombed, I'd talk to mothers there who'd say things like, 'We're trying to look for wood to burn to heat milk for our babies, they keep bombing us and there's no power, sister.' But then I'd make a point of speaking to settlers in Sderot who've had to go to their bomb shelters when Hamas rockets hit. At the same time children in Gaza were being killed by one of the most powerful militaries in the world.

The loss of a child is an unimaginable tragedy. One that I've witnessed many times in my line of work but have no way of fully understanding. All I know is that when it comes to a parent burying their son or daughter, it doesn't matter which side of the conflict you're on. In the course of my work, I've listened to many Israeli settlers talk to me about their real fear when the rockets strike their areas. While Palestinian families have no access to panic rooms or bomb shelters and if houses are shelled, entire families can be wiped out.

One of (my husband) Ahmed's friends from Gaza was living in London at the time but his fiancée was stuck there during the 2008 conflict and he didn't know if she was going to make it. I remember one evening all of us just sitting in his flat, his head down staring at the floor. Ahmed, trying to make conversation and break the silence. Me, asking silly questions … 'So, how's everyone, back home? Have you heard from them?' and then I'd stop myself. Because none of those questions had easy answers at that moment. If anything, they made him more anxious.

While this conflict has been etched in my mind two things are clear:

1) On a personal level, I've avoided conversations and debates about it for as long as I can remember. This issue is and has always been so fraught and controversial – I still find it deeply confusing at times.

2) It's impossible for me to hate or judge anyone because of their religion, even though I've been judged many times because of mine.

Take your dad's story. This man, who exposed himself to hardship to help others when he could've had an easy comfortable life. I wonder what would've happened if you told your dad's story to that class of young men in Doha. What would they have said about this pharmacist who helped black South Africans get access to medicine? And what if you told them he was a Jew?

I love you always.

# 10.

# SHELLEY

I love you too. So much. Over time and space and across continents. We live in this crazy world, forced to draw and obey lines between countries, tribes, families; pitted against one another by forces we can't control. The longer I live, the more I believe that our so-called enemies are nothing more than our own images of fear that we attack in blind panic.

My mother told me she stopped going to Shul at about thirteen. My stepdad, whom she married in her twenties, was also born Jewish. But they got married in a church. Later, we celebrated Christmas.

As I grew up, I feared and resisted what I saw as inherited physical Jewish traits that I saw in my extended family: heavy dark hair; puppy fat; a scary potential to look like my grandfather's thick-set and troll-like sisters, Aunty Janey and Aunty Katy.

When I was eleven, I asked to be christened in a church in South Africa. I even chose my own godparents. Later I was confirmed, in the same church, in the name of Jesus Christ, Amen. Somewhere in my late teens, I felt an exhaustion come over me.

I shrugged off any religious leanings like tired clothes. I held on to a deeper, more formless and expansive sense of spirituality. One that was never tied to laws, or rules or traditions.

When I was ten, a little black girl was adopted into my family and grew up with me and my brothers as our beloved sibling. Living under apartheid in a family that was essentially acting criminally – because it was illegal for different races to live together under the same roof – sharpened my experiences of injustice. My mother was kicked out of parks for taking her children – of different races – to play on the swings. We could not go on holiday together because black people were not allowed. Those were the small things. I thought, all this division, all this hatred, this them-and-us dichotomy, war across the world, in the name of religion, or faith; all this death, in the name of racial supremacy; all this fighting, for boundaries, for power. Us and them. Self and Other.

Jews had a complex position in South Africa. During and after World War Two, they were perceived as a significantly suspect 'other'. When I was a child, Jews had only been considered 'white' for a few decades and while some Jews aligned themselves with the nationalist government after the war, they were over-represented in the fight against apartheid. A disproportionate number of those of Jews, maybe unsurprisingly, became social activists, working to end the suffering of black people who were the victims of atrocities at the hands of the white National Party.

I was awoken early to social injustice.

No matter how many times I write this out, or dream it, I am haunted by the things I saw on any ordinary day growing up in South Africa. I may have seen this ten times, or a thousand times, but in my mind it is there forever: in the traffic on any given day after school, a yellow police van stacked full of black people, arrested for not having a 'pass' or being in the wrong place under the laws of Influx Control. The abuse of power. Human beings doing no harm, at the mercy of the powerful, the legislators, those who decide who is free and who is not, and why. I stared into the hollow, yellow eyes of the captured men and women, nannies, gardeners – people who I interacted with on a daily basis – in a parallel world of hell in an afternoon traffic jam.

I wanted an escape. From history. From geography. Just as they did.

I didn't want to be positioned by politics or religion or skin colour.

At school I fell in love with a German boy and as a result I wanted to learn German. My very Jewish grandmother was horrified. 'It's a terrible language,' she said. 'So many of our people died in the war. How can you?'

I shrugged. I yearned to speak German. I studied it at school and when I was fifteen, I went to Germany for six months. There I lived with a family who treated me like Cinderella. The woman was verbally abusive and I cleaned house for her eternally dissatisfied disposition. It was only thirty-five years after the end of World War Two and I didn't yet understand the story that slept beneath my skin – I didn't know that these stories of trauma and dispossession were already running in my veins. My great-grandfather and mother were refugees who had fled pogroms and persecution in 1914. I feel primed to sense danger and threat and then to run, long before a situation becomes obviously dangerous.

It was like this in Germany. I knew I had to escape the Cinderella household. A kind family rescued me and were loving and generous. When I told them my story, revealed my history, they were quiet. The father of the family said he had been a member of the Hitler Youth. Just thirty-five years earlier and I would have been taken to a concentration camp. He was on the side of those people who killed my people and so were his family. He said no one thought there was anything wrong with their position back then. It was only later that they considered that they had been part of something unspeakable.

This couple took me in and cared for me, and loved me, and still do. He's in his nineties now, and we still call each other. I learned German fluently and spoke it without an accent in five months.

When I returned from Germany to South Africa, my grandmother was horrified to hear the language falling effortlessly from my tongue. Those people – she said – were the worst of humanity. But later I discovered that her father spoke Yiddish – and Yiddish (Jewish) is a German dialect – so maybe it already sat there waiting in my DNA.

Ashkenazi Jews, Christians, Germans, Arabs, Muslims. What sets us against each other is written by our own hands. After World War Two, after the demise of apartheid, after the Berlin Wall came down, how do we listen to our hearts rather than perpetuate the endless fallacy of us and them, self and other?

None of that othering makes any of us more human – and no one wins.

*

When I came into the classroom that day, and Bassel showed me the bullet wound from the Israeli soldier, it was unbearable. He may have wanted to kill me if he knew that my heritage was Jewish, but I am as far from that soldier as the most distant part of the universe is from earth. I'm a Jew, because of my heritage. And a Christian, because of my eleven-year-old-self's choice. And you, one of my most-loved people in the world, are Muslim. And I adore you.

I can imagine how impossible it must feel to have to remain impartial in those circumstances you describe. How do you even process these events? The position that accidents of birth (and therefore religion and culture and geography) put us in can cause such a fracturing of self: I'm a South African — I was seen as 'white', the same colour as the oppressor, in the 1980s. But before I was born, in 1930s South Africa, Jews were not-white. At all. Later, after apartheid legislation, along with Lebanese and Greek South Africans, Jews were classified as 'white' — even as pervasive anti-Semitism infused much of the Afrikaner disposition towards them.

I grew up then, in a family of black and now-white people. I was born Jewish, so how could I love German, the language of the oppressor, those murderers of Jewish people? But I did. I loved them. Even the very father, who as a young man may have believed that Jews were the scourge of the earth and needed to be obliterated. I lived in Qatar and I met Bassel and he broke my heart because he looked like my younger brother — because there is shared genetic heritage. Because we are so similar. We are each other.

*Shalom Alechem; Salaam Alaykum.*

The love and friendship and regard that we have, Shaimz, is impervious to the histories others insist are written in some indelible text.

But I was younger and perhaps naïve in Doha — and as my young women students told me, 'Mrs Shelley, you are older than we are, but in so many ways we know more than you do.'

# 11.

# SHAIMAA

One of the things that drew me to you as a teacher and later as a friend is that very thing your students commented on. Your ability to hold on to a youthful spirit. By the time you'd reached Doha, you'd had your fair share of turmoil. Yes, you found love, but it feels to me that it didn't come easy. You lived in fear of your life every day for good reason. Your friends and friends of friends were killed. It feels to me that the *living* in South Africa seemed to be constantly impacted with the dying everywhere. You ran with your loved one and endured financial hardship together and when you finally got to a place that was going to secure a regular income you realised quickly that it came at a price. And yet through all of that you have this inner light about you. This determination to move forward, this unrelenting curiosity that I'm so in awe of. This was enough to age the most buoyant of people and yet your spirit remained intact in its youthful resilience despite your years, brushing with these young beautiful women who aged long before their time. I believe among many other things, what they identified in you is that gentle strength – the refusal to give up hope, something I believe many of these women at Qatar University had. Even if

59

they didn't know it. Your innocence would have amused them I'm sure, but there's also a sadness in what they told you, because in a way it's an admission that they lost theirs. The reasons would take a lifetime to understand.

*

Despite all that, I still sometimes find it fascinating that you too are a runaway. Like me. A nomad like me. Like other women like me. And the more I knew about where you grew up and what you saw around you every single day the more I understood why you needed to leave. It's amazing. In a way both our surroundings were trying to stifle us. Both were geared for us to stop existing as we were.

Our writing together has allowed us both to look inward, to go to those locked doors in mouldy corridors and not only acknowledge what's behind them but also bring it into the light and share it. Sometimes we don't know what we need to do until we start doing it.

# 12.

# SHELLEY

You are the window through which my eyes are permitted to look into a world that breaks my heart and shatters me. But your voice illuminates my life and gives me hope. Your loving friendship heals generations of invisible damage. Thank you for allowing me to be. I want human beings to be different. I want a world in which the strong protect the weak, the sick, the vulnerable. I want a world in which women are seen and treated with profound respect, every day, in every part of the world.

*

We had been in Qatar for three months when I fell pregnant with Tim. This was the first time Paul and I had had any sort of stable income and though there was no real solid ground to stand on – we had no 'home' we felt we would go back to eventually, unlike the other expats – this was as stable as we'd ever been.

Almost immediately the nausea started. Not just a bit of queasiness. I felt like I'd been poisoned. My sense of smell was acute. When I went to teach my students on the women's side, suddenly all I could smell was perfume as crowds of students poured into the classroom. I would have to duck out of class to take a deep breath and deal with the waves of nausea.

Driving along the Corniche was unbearable. The few bits of grass that were visible at roundabouts were watered with grey water. The smell was gut-churning. It permeated the universe. I wanted to vomit up the whole place – roads, roundabouts particularly, flats, swimming pools, cars. It was hard to eat anything.

Manal's engagement party happened on a weekend. Being pregnant challenged me. Every smell, every movement made me nauseated. It was early evening, and Paul took me to the villa in a suburb of Doha I'd never visited before. High-walled homes with gates, the outside lit in the orange glow of a lamp. The sound of music drifted through the air.

'Pick me up around nine?' I said.

I'd never been to such an event, and I knew that perhaps I never would again. The courtyard adjoining the villa was lit with coloured fairy lights. I entered through a cast-iron gate and immediately the smell of cooking lamb or goat made me feel sick. I thought I might pass out.

A long table stood in the courtyard, overflowing with meats and rice and flat breads and yoghurts and dishes with familiar aromas.

Manal was Palestinian by heritage.

There is much shared history in Jewish and Palestinian cooking.

Manal was unrecognisable. I'd never seen her shiny dark hair down her back. I'd never seen her eyes rimmed with kohl. She wore a beautiful turquoise dress and she danced, her hips moving like a swaying crescent moon. Arabic music played. A nine- or ten-year-old girl danced. Manal's little sister. Her movements were already sophisticated and controlled. Her midriff and bangles caught the flashing fairy lights. Her eyes shone. Mothers and grandmothers and aunts sat and watched the young girls dancing. I stood near them, knowing no one, in awe of the expertise of these young dancers, wondering who taught them, where they practised, stunned by the difference between the abaya-covered expression of femininity at the university and what revealed itself beneath the purple sky and upside-down Arabian moon.

I began to understand. The women, free of any male gaze, could be themselves. The watching mothers and grandmothers were match-making in their minds, picking out future brides for sons, and the girls knew this; even the little ones, unaware of the deeper subtext, danced as if auditioning for starring roles.

The men, I learned, were having a separate party.

I was mesmerised by the exquisite dresses, the dark rimmed eyes, glistening skin, a sensual contrast to the austere heaviness, the covered and hidden versions of girls that I encountered at the university.

Manal looked beautiful. I wished silently that she would be treated well. I hoped whoever married her would treasure her. She was still a child. Her eyes shimmered with hope and romantic dreams. An image of Manal and her time-travelling Keats played in my mind.

When I said goodbye to her, she thanked me, and went back to dancing, and I watched the swirl of energy in her step and prayed that married life would not take that away from her.

*

The poems that the women students read out in the class after we'd completed *Ship or Sheep* sounded as though they had been written with all the romantic idealism of a lost era. None of them would have been out of place in Wordsworth's and Keats's

England, read on a windy knoll on the Isle of Wight or on a beach in Brighton.

Sometimes after that, in some of my classes, but not in all (I taught five repeats of the same class), students wrote and shared poetry. We did not do this on a regular basis and I saw it as a reprieve, a small break in the relentless phonetics and phonology program. I sensed tension around the writing of individual creative pieces, but it didn't stop us doing it.

Several weeks after Manal's engagement, and soon after her wedding, I began to notice that many of the students in your class were pregnant. At eighteen, maybe half the class were already in arranged marriages, so Manal's was no exception. I wondered how married life was for her, and I hoped she was okay. She looked pale and perhaps subdued. After class one afternoon, air conditioners blasting freezing air into the room, I was about to leave when Manal came to me. 'Mrs Shelley. I'm pregnant.'

I was shocked.

Paul and I were together for a few years before we married, and more years after that before I was pregnant. This seemed dizzyingly sudden.

'Oh, goodness. Congratulations!'

She smiled, but the smile did not reach her eyes. She was eighteen. I was twenty-eight and I felt too young. I tried to imagine how in a few short weeks, a teenager went from being innocent and childlike, dreaming of meeting John Keats on a plane, to married and pregnant – her life's story already written in its entirety. Was I projecting my vivid imagination onto her, or had the texture of her future dreams changed so much that I read the absence of hope in her face?

Did she read my uncertainty? When she spoke, again she sounded like the older, wiser person giving comfort to me. 'I'm happy. My mother-in-law is happy. I only hope I will have a boy. Then my husband will be happy. It's as it should be, Mrs Shelley.'

She was such a good student and she was going to do her best to be a good wife.

'Take care of yourself, Manal.'

'I will. Thank you Mrs Shelley. And you.'

'You're so welcome. See you next week.'

But I did not see her the next week. Nor ever again.

*

By December of that first year, our class was swimming in a sea of oestrogen. I could not tell who was pregnant for quite some time because abayas are good at hiding everything.

One by one, students began to return after giving birth. One morning, Salma, who'd just had her baby three days ago, stayed after class. She had charcoal rings under her eyes and her face was puffy. She did not look like the sparkly self she had been just a week before.

'Salma, why are you back so soon? Where's your baby?'

'At home with my mother.'

'Are you okay?' I was thinking, she's not breastfeeding then, and she's not staying home with her tiny newborn baby ...

She shook her head. 'Mrs Shelley,' she said. 'Don't have your baby here.'

'What happened?'

'They messed me up down there. Now I must go to England to have surgery. It's bad, very bad.' Her eyes filled with tears. 'So that's why I won't be back for next term – maybe for a long time.'

There were no words in my vocabulary for that situation. I took a nauseous breath. 'Thanks for telling me that. I'll think carefully about where I have my baby.'

What had they 'messed up'?

It took me years to understand what sometimes happened to some of those young women when they went to give birth. But

I'd already decided that if it was the last thing I did, I'd leave the country to have my baby, even if it meant going back to South Africa, where my fellow countrymen were being murdered in car hijackings alone at a rate of around 50 a day.

*

Being pregnant gave me a sudden and special entry card to an exclusive club that I did not know existed. Girls came to me after class, huddled together in small groups, to share their stories.

'Gaia's husband wouldn't even stop with sex even when it was her period,' Salwa said.

'When Maryam got married her mother-in-law and aunt held her down and held her legs open while her husband practically raped her.'

'I've been for three rounds of IVF and if the next round doesn't work, my husband's going to look for a second wife.'

I looked from one childlike face to another.

'Mrs Shelley, if you have your baby in the hospital, make sure you don't land in the ward under where they leave the illegal babies to die. One of the students said that the ghosts of the other babies and the real babies never stop crying,' Salwa said.

'What illegal babies?'

They looked at me as if I'd asked a stupid question.

'The men who rape the Filipino maids – when the maids get pregnant, they go in to give birth and the babies are taken away and the rumour is, the babies are left to die. Then the maids go straight back to work and then it happens again. So, the rumour is that there is a ward where they leave the babies.'

I wanted to disbelieve them, and the possibility of a ward for illegal babies left to die.

A Polish colleague at work who had recently had a baby talked to me one day after classes – talked about the hospital, about birth, and I told her the rumour. 'Is there any truth to this?' She said she had a Filipino maid and from her she learned that there were cases that essentially amounted to slavery in Doha. That there were Filipino women there who worked seven-day weeks as maids for wealthy local families. Their passports were confiscated, she said, and they couldn't leave, because their wages were withheld. They were often raped by their employers, and their babies … I will never know the real story, but it was enough to make me decide that I was going to have my baby back in South Africa.

Something fierce was growing under my skin. How could I not come to desperately love these girl-women, to want to spirit them away from their luxurious, gilded empty lives that I eventually came to know when I was invited to engagement parties, or on the rare occasion I tutored one or two local female students. I could leave and have my baby anywhere. They couldn't.

In some universe where this exists as just a story, you are the one who got away. You are the hope. You showed how a girl could do it: run away. Have a voice. Free yourself. And later, give voice to thousands of others.

We were twin souls but I didn't know it yet. I'd been running my whole life: I resisted being seen as a white South African representing apartheid South Africa in my multi-racial home; I didn't want to be the Jew in Germany, nor the Jew whom Bassel might want to kill. I didn't want to be a woman first, and a human being after. And even now, I don't want the projections, the ascribed position, the representational art that can be made of me, to exist in my wake when I walk out of a room, or a country.

For a long time now we've been running in parallel, together.

# 13.

# SHAIMAA

I remember feeling shocked when I saw a colleague of mine visibly pregnant while we were still in our second year of university. I asked myself how that was okay, how it was normal that a girl as young as me was going to be a mother. We would've been in our late teens.

I was still struggling with things like which classes to enrol in for the coming semester and how to avoid certain professors and their subjects. What to do for fun and how to face the deeply un-fun reality of being a young woman in Doha. How short my sleeves could be before I got caught by the university patrol women officers. Boys. How to meet them and how not to get caught. I was not thinking about husbands, and definitely not children.

*

The workings of social and marital life within a Qatari family were a mystery to me. I really couldn't fathom it. From day one, the covered-up women, the houses with the high walls and the segregated campuses made it impossible to fully understand what was on the other side, even though technically I was on the other side. In my ten years in Doha, I was invited to weddings and dinner parties and a number of other all-female gatherings at a few Qatari friends' houses. And while my hosts were very generous and welcoming, I always felt like an outsider. I appreciated their hospitality and enjoyed their company but didn't quite get how these households worked. It was quite different from where I grew up.

*

The veneer of linguistic or cultural familiarity made living in Doha very confusing. Because under the crust of Qatar being an Arab, Muslim country – where I recognised the language but had trouble with the very different accent – it was like being on a different planet.

I know you felt the same but I guess your sense of alienation came from the starkness of contrasts.

Mine was more about navigating the gradations of differences. Doha's arid and monotonous landscape with its spacious newly built villas and apartments made me realise how rich and diverse the scenery and the architecture were in my home town.

My mother used to always tell me that you can never get lost in Alexandria. Wherever you are, just get yourself to the sea. Follow the promenade and you'll be able to find your way.

The sea wasn't just the sound and smell and vista of my childhood. It was also my inner compass. My sense of being at home.

My fondest memories are of playing in the sand with my cousins. Back before us girls were told that we were no longer allowed to wear swimsuits and bare skin.

I knew Alexandria was a historically diverse metropolitan city before I knew what that actually meant. There were Greek,

Italian, Armenian, Egyptian, Jewish, French and Turkish communities.

I grew up with famous French cafes like Trianon and Delices Café in Raml station, downtown. Gerbis was the name of the Greek shop where my grandma got her milk and where my dad used to get us the best rice pudding in the world.

Some of my favourite songs are those of Sayed Darwish, a famous and beloved Alexandrian musician and composer.

European architecture was everywhere in historical areas like Mansheya.

Unfortunately these buildings have been so poorly kept and many have been razed to the ground in favour of tall developments with expensive apartments.

Alexandria is battling for its soul but it *has* soul.

Doha was much cleaner. Better maintained. The Corniche was beautiful. But there was an emptiness to it all. A blandness.

Our apartment in Doha was three times the size of ours in Alexandria. And while I appreciated having my own room and AC, I knew I was confined.

In Alexandria we lived in an average neighbourhood, the ground floor flat I grew up in with my sister and our parents was small with not much sunlight.

But a few minutes' walk and you're right by the promenade, smelling the sea.

A 30-minute drive to the east was the Al Montaza Palace and Gardens, which used to be King Farouk's summerhouse, a beautiful expanse of green spaces with the beach to one side. My sister and I used to run around those gardens with our cousins.

A drive in the opposite direction took you to El Raml district and then old Alexandria beyond till you reached the Citadel of Qaitbay.

A few tram stations just before El Raml was the centre of my world – and in my eyes the whole universe.

This was my childhood house. Not our own, but my grandma's and even though my grandfather was alive and very much a big presence in my growing up, it was my grandmother who gave this house life.

This is where I'd play in the street for hours with the other children in the building and the buildings nearby, with my grandparents looking on from their balcony.

It was a big apartment on the first floor. But what I loved most about it was that light. The sun entered from its many windows all day long and it always felt open and fresh.

My childhood was the beach and this house, which is all the sadder that it only lasted till I was ten. It wasn't so much that my childhood ended than it was stolen. After the age of ten the streets where I played became the frontlines I had to survive.

I wish I had more childhood.

All of that made landing and living in Doha feel like adjusting to a different palate of senses. It took a while to get used to a new level of confinement and conservatism. To new limitations. It was made that much harder by the fact that I'd just finished high school and was about to start university in Alexandria and get a small taste of some autonomy, of going to classes on my own instead of a school bus and of course being in a co-education environment.

But instead, I found myself snatched away from that and plonked into the women's building in Qatar University, looking for a portacabin that would be the home of my Islamic Studies 101 core course for the first semester. The flipside of that was that this was an ideal environment for me to excel. The classes weren't crowded – I studied what I loved: English literature and linguistics. And for the first time in my life – straight As! Even if that lasted only briefly.

I would later learn to navigate and appreciate my life in this small city. After the shock of leaving everything and everyone I knew, I realised Qatar offered a space, comfort and a lifestyle that I would never find in my home country. But for all it offered, our host country had its fair share of small daily perils.

Egyptian streets were hazardous and still are, but they were an open battlefield. You went out knowing that, and you armoured up and fended for yourself. You were harassed, howled at, touched and humiliated (all of the above on bad days) but it was all out there. Expected. The minute you stepped into public space, the beast was ready, and you were game. There are lucky escapes but there's no safety.

In Doha there was a facade of safety and simplicity. But that soon gave way to a very different but equally sinister form of harassment. The streets weren't safe, they were just empty and I, you and women like us who didn't cover from head to toe, were easily spotted and targeted. Those men driving fast, fancy cars with a great sense of entitlement. Not only are you a woman and not covered, you're a non-native, obviously there for a job and so in need of making a living, which automatically puts you in a lower category than a native woman. Not that they get a better deal.

The most troubling and fascinating thing about being in the Gulf is that for me it was a different shade of living in the Middle East. Yes, I was Arabic-speaking and came from the oldest and most enduring culture in the region, but I was still an outsider.

It's amazing the insight you got into those women's lives. I never got those stories – I guess they saw you as a Class A outsider and also wanted to 'educate' you and take you in a little.

\*

There's always been a complicated dynamic between Egyptian expats working in the Gulf and locals. Our culture is loved and revered throughout the region. And yet, economically millions of Egyptian labourers, workers, teachers, doctors, engineers and many other professionals had flocked to the Gulf countries in the seventies, eighties and nineties to make a better living. That created a tension that confused and flustered me. The upside was that as an Egyptian you get embraced into these cultures by virtue of your accent and background. You represent what these men and women watch on TV. You're an ambassador of Egyptian pop culture just by being Egyptian. And yes, we do have the sharpest sense of humour in the region!

When they (Gulf Arabs) speak to you, they imagine their favourite film or TV series. In its most crass sense, your presence is entertaining. I'd like to think that some of these women liked my company because they just saw someone who was different from them, but whom they could also relate to.

Whenever I got invited to weddings and engagement parties or got shown photos of these girls' babies in class, something inside me would whisper, 'NOT ME! Not ever. My family wouldn't do this. I'd never be arranged to marry someone – that's what they do here …' But it was only a matter of time.

My parents were dismissive of girls being engaged or married while they were in school or university. They were insistent that our education was non-negotiable. But the minute we stepped out into the real world, the countdown started, and I didn't even know it! It was also around the time my dad died so all eyes were on me (being the eldest) and my mum, and what was clearly to become the next step.

I remember how excited she was breaking the news to me that a family friend wanted to marry me. I'd never seen her as enthusiastic as she was explaining how ideal he was, because, 'We know who he is and who his family is, and he also lives in the States. Which is what you want isn't it?'

I was so conflicted. I felt myself being encircled and hijacked and I gave in. The sense of approval. Of making my mother happy. Of doing the right thing. And the USA prospect. All pushed me.

But then I froze. The day before the engagement, after we'd already picked the rings and I picked a dress, I completely froze and couldn't go ahead with it. Call it the Hand of God, call it gut feeling ... I just couldn't do it. I was suffocated and felt trapped.

For the first time I had to face the wrath of not just my mother but my whole family, even though it was my mother's words that hurt the most.

One night she woke me up and told me how I'd disappointed her, how all her toiling over the years to educate and protect us had come to nothing. Basically, I brought shame upon them because I'd changed my mind and somehow, I was going to pay for that. There are many other details, but the gist is that I'd let everyone down. They were waiting for a moment of happiness after my dad died, and I'd denied them that.

Remember, you asked about when my dad died and if there was a chance that his family would take custody of me and my sister? I don't know about the legality of it to be honest, but I do know that a mother's custody of her own children, whether a widow or a divorcee, is scrutinised only if she has a relationship with someone – then she's deemed unfit and her children could be taken away.

But when this engagement fell through, my sister floated this as a possibility. I don't know if she was really worried, or if it was meant to scare me back to my senses. I remember her saying in my mum's presence: 'Look, what you've done is shocking and I'm now seriously worried that the family will start to question how Mum has been raising us. They might want to take over. I'm scared.'

That really shook me. That in a decision I made about my own life, I had possibly given up more of myself to other people to decide my life for me!

None of that happened, thankfully. I still wonder whether my sister did that because she was genuinely worried, or because my family told her to say so.

Either way, it brought home this gnawing feeling of my life not being mine. There was always, *always* someone who was going to make decisions for me. And my capacity to make any decisions was limited to the set of boundaries that were already decided for me. It physically hurt me. Something broke inside me at the time. But something else took its place ...

I was done with chasing the approval of others. Of proving that I was worthy and for marriage to be the only barometer of that. When we arrived in Doha after that visit, I knew that my life needed to be mine even though I was nowhere near making that happen.

I was just never going to go through that again. Not that this stopped my family from putting me through what seemed like endless arranged meetings with possible suitors both in Egypt and in Qatar. The more I resisted, the harder it became. One day I told my mother I wanted to try for a journalism MA at Columbia University in the USA. I was going on and on about how unlikely but wonderful it would be. I don't remember the exact conversation, but I think it went something like this.

'Then what?'

'What do you mean? Then I'd have a Masters in Journalism,' I said.

'Then what?'

'Well, I'd try to find a job maybe here at Al Jazeera or somewhere else, I don't know.'

'And go and live on your own?'

Then the conversation stopped.

Then she said: 'Why don't you get married and do what you want!'

'I don't want to get married. I want to study.'

I honestly don't remember how the rest of it went. But I do remember two things that she said because they're etched in my memory: 'You're just an ordinary girl, Shaimaa. You'll marry an ordinary man.'

(I think in an attempt to get me to settle and manage my expectations.)

And: 'What is it that you do with your life? You just work.'

I wanted to shout. What was all this education for? What was the point in you trying to build our characters? What was all that about work ethic, independence, diligence? Why have you gone back on everything you taught us? Or is that even what you taught us?

To this day I still wish I could say that to Mum. To this day I believe I am a big disappointment to her, adding to the list of things and actions she disapproved of. To this day I wonder why this still bothers me.

# 14.

# SHELLEY

It sinks into my soul, your description of Egyptian streets as an open battlefield. I can hardly imagine you as a five-year-old, a ten-year-old, having to make sense of that world, of your place in it. How long did your innocence last?

I realise I know precious little about your broken engagement. You were so young and full of hopes and dreams despite the people you loved the most doing everything they could, it seemed, to keep you in your place – for your own, and their safety. I get that. And I know it was a big deal, but only in the way those who have *no idea*, might know. How might your life have panned out had you gone ahead with that union? In every way, that young act of yours was a warrior move – an act of massive courage and defiance. People the world over have no idea. The shock of it hits me now. This happened to you, my sweet-faced Shaimaa, who was so brilliant and funny and sassy and down-to-earth. You were going to be married to some stranger. The risks of girls like you saying no play out in an understory that we never hear. Men the world over have *no idea*.

Troubling are the way statistics paint a certain picture. The invisible crimes, the ones that aren't reported, have nowhere to go.

From smarttraveller.com:

**Is Qatar safe for ladies?**
**Safety**. Doha is a very **safe** city for visitors and has very little crime. **Women** walking alone might be approached or may be the object of curiosity. Just be polite and continue on your way.

An object of curiosity.

Be polite.

For me, to grow up in South Africa was to be formed by the constant threat of apex predators. There are tawny-eyed lions and cheetahs and panthers – all of them prey on the weak, the young, the vulnerable of other species. But they do this for survival, and it's the natural way of things. So by far the most terrifying predators to me were the human ones – those who also preyed on the weak, the young and the vulnerable of their own species, but who did and do it for pleasure, for power, for some sick gain. In South Africa when I was growing up, the murder rate got so high that sometime in the 1990s they stopped publishing crime statistics. Now it's suggested that South Africans are still dying at a rate of at least 50 people a day from violent crime.

To be a woman in South Africa is to live with the shadow of stories of rape, both in the news or in your close circles. The threat always feels present and real even if it hasn't happened to you. Another stark statistic was that one in three people are HIV positive. Put those two together and any woman would understand the desire to run away. I learned early on that Africa was a continent with very little mercy.

So it's maybe surprising that I would choose to go back there to give birth to Tim.

But the choice was an impossible one. The Gulf, as you said, was overshadowed by my thoughts of the ghosts of dead babies and traumatised mothers that wafted into my dreams, fed by rumours and the haunted eyes of my students. I think these young women told me their stories because we were together in the 'married club' and 'mother-to-be-club'. If you tell those stories to those who haven't gone down that track yet, you might scare them, be responsible for, I don't know, a revolution of unmarried teenagers?

A conspiracy of silence by women, for women, existed for sure.

After their stories I thought, at least in South Africa I could have my baby on my terms – even if I'd have to not wear a seat belt or put my baby in a car seat on the way back from the hospital for fear of being hijacked. There were stories in South Africa of cars being hijacked, of mothers held up at gunpoint, and criminals driving off with babies and children strapped into their car seats.

When you're running from the frying pan, it's all too easy to land in the fire.

I ran away from South Africa and landed, after years of running, in the Middle East. I coveted safety and stability; I wasn't looking for adventure. I wanted a steady income, and to not live in fear.

But then I had to decide where to give birth to Tim.

And I ran from Qatar back to South Africa, because I feared the insidious beast more than the overtly predatory one.

Eighteen-year-old Maryam's final comment after she'd had her baby made my decision to leave Qatar to give birth final.

'When I was in labour,' she said, 'I was in so much pain. I was crying for my mother. The doctor shouted at me and slapped my face and my legs and told me to shut up and grow up.'

Qatar is a very safe place for ladies.

I chose the risk of armed robbery, rape, hijacking, even murder, above Maryam's experience.

In Qatar at the time and as far as I knew, no husbands were allowed with their wives when they gave birth, no matter who they were.

I've discovered recently in my research as an academic that there are high rates of depression and suicidal ideation in young girls in the Gulf – that they display a sense of hopelessness and despair about their futures. The highest contributing factor for depression in a recent study in the United Arab Emirates, which is more liberal than Qatar, is ... being female.

In 2017, a study showed a third of adolescents between 13 and 17 in Qatar had depression – women were significantly more affected.

*

I had to leave before the end of the semester to have my baby, because after 32 weeks of pregnancy, I would not be allowed to fly. Even though the teaching was over, we weren't supposed to leave until a specific date. Paul was allowed to sign my exit visa. To let me go. As his wife, I was his charge. So, he did. And he flew with me from Doha to Dubai because it would not be easy to fly between Doha and Dubai as a single, pregnant woman, without risking serious harassment. I needed a male chaperone.

Once in Dubai, we said goodbye and Paul flew back to Qatar, while I broke university rules because I did not want to be stuck in Doha and prevented from getting out.

Immediately, international passengers offered help. A young man gave up his seat to me in the waiting lounge; another, with his own family, helped me get my bags into the overhead locker in the plane.

Paul arrived in South Africa three weeks later. I'd grown huge and uncomfortable but I trusted my body, that it would know what to do, how to push a whole human being out from under my heart.

It was early spring in South Africa. News item on page four: *Pregnant mother shot dead in front of four-year-old by armed intruders.*

She'd made the mistake of reaching for a panic button.

Friday night we returned, Paul and I, with my parents, to the house I spent my youth in, from a movie.

There were eleven or twelve intruders on the property, making their way down towards the fence at the bottom, carrying computers, suitcases, household goods. They were a group of squatters from an informal settlement a few blocks away on the river.

I thought we would be killed that night as we stood there in the dark and as I tried to remember the police phone number.

I thought, this is a recurring nightmare I've had but I know I can't wake myself from this one. What on earth possessed me to come back here to have a baby?

The police force arrived eventually: a single, trembling young man who assured me he would not be making any arrests as there was no one at the police station to take fingerprints. He shot at the intruders. They dropped what they were carrying and leapt over the fence, heading back to the river.

A week later, I gave birth to Tim in a home-birth unit in the Bedford Gardens Hospital with a midwife at my side.

The pain was so bad that I wished I could die.

I understood how thin the veil is between death and birth.

My mother was by my side, and my husband.

And even with all the love and care surrounding me, I still wanted to die.

In the middle of a contraction, my husband's arms were around me, my mother's whisper was in my ear and I thought of Maryam and I couldn't breathe.

'I can't do this,' I said.

My mum told me to blow into a paper bag because my lips were going blue.

# 15.

# SHAIMAA

I just want to reach out to you in my head and hold your hand and tell you I come from the future and all this suffering is going to end and that this baby is going to grow up into this beautiful, talented young man who plays music and flies planes and has so much love inside him. One of the things I never went into detail about with my sister was the birth part of her three children. It's just something I try to block from my head. Giving birth is definitely one of the many reasons I don't want children (something I've never dared say out loud in front of my family).

*

To think of young Maryam, who was still in many ways a child, having a child of her own, being denied the basic right to feel pain. All alone with no support and then to be slapped around and ordered to grow up, to get that child out of her – then she's expected to love it and take care of it after it caused her so much agony! I can imagine the horror you felt when you heard that – a horror that sent you packing to a lesser horror.

\*

This gave me chills …

*'It was early spring in South Africa. News item on page four:
pregnant mother shot dead in front of four-year-old by armed
intruders …'*

You went back home for relative support and safety and yet this
was on your mind! This and the prospect of your baby being
snatched. To be pregnant and having to call the police to get
intruders out of your house!

To get yourself ready to give life while fearing for your own.
It's like these stories we cover about having babies in warzones –
you were in one. I remember wanting to ask you this when I
spoke about Egyptian streets feeling like a battlefield, which they
absolutely are … But with you in many ways it was a literal
battle. Did you think about that every day? If you or one of your
family members were going to be held at gun-point? Shot? How
do you process that fear? How do you function when you're the
colour of the oppressor but you're not the oppressor?

\*

Doha memories elude me often now. By the time I left, it had
lost any redeeming features of its small simple self. We moved
to Doha in 1996 and I left in 2006. More women were in
the workplace – I can't put my finger on it exactly but there
was a definite shift. Women and girls were more visible, even
though Qatar remained a conservative place. There was a huge
drive towards education in general and support for women in
particular. I remember when my female Qatari friends were
finally allowed to drive and what a big deal that was. Years

before Saudi women. I remember one of my Qatari lecturers at university back in the mid-nineties saying that she couldn't go abroad to finish her post-grad studies because the men in her family who could accompany her (her father or brothers) could not travel at the time. Now women are able to get scholarships and travel. It's progress no doubt. I wouldn't be able to tell you if that translated into real change in their social lives.

On the other hand though ... In that time, buildings grew taller, malls bigger and the city more crowded and less peaceful. There was a Doha boom for sure. But for me it was slowly losing its spirit.

The Qatari government–funded and hugely powerful and popular Al Jazeera news channel had placed the country prominently on the pan-Arab media and diplomacy map. And in 2006 Al Jazeera English was about to launch. The Education City university complex with Carnegie Mellon and Georgetown University campuses had risen in the desert ready to usher in a new era of expensive overseas education at home. Preparations for the Asian Games were underway and the whole city felt like it was coming of age, even if it was trying too hard to be like Dubai. While there were more 'options', Doha was getting even more suffocating for me than it was when it was a small city with one mall and a couple of good restaurants.

Ahmed was getting ready to leave for London to start his job at BBC Arabic. We'd worked together at QBS and became friends (and a bit more) three years before we got married.

One night when I found out he was leaving, I called him and told him how angry I was that he was going to leave without saying goodbye!

'We had a fight, remember? You stopped talking to me!' he said.

'So?!' I yelled.

'So I didn't think you cared what I did or where I went,' he said.

'You idiot! Of course I cared. I've always cared,' I said.

We agreed to spend the two weeks before he left for London together because 'we didn't know when we'd see each other again'.

Then one day he said, 'I want you to come with me.'

I look back at those days now and marvel at how fast it all happened. How I packed up my ten years in Doha, hugged my mum and sister and said goodbye. The first time ever I'd be separated from them long-term. The first time I'd have a life that didn't involve them.

I love so many things about my hubby including his timing at that very moment. It was impeccable!

Leaving Doha was hard. But it was exactly what I needed. I'm still baffled by that facade of abundance and safety that the Gulf (including Qatar of course) projects. This idea that people can shop their problems away. I remember being in Saudi Arabia during the Arab Spring in 2011 when there were whispers of possible protests on the streets of Riyadh. Of course, on the day nothing happened, and we journalists were bussed around a few streets and told, 'Look. All quiet,' by the police. Then we were told by our local fixer that there's no way 'we could be like Egypt, Libya or Syria or even Bahrain. God forbid!'

What she meant was the vacuum, the chaos that ensues when wars go on for too long or when dictators are ousted and leave a rancid gaping hole of conflict and corruption that only another extreme power can fill.

'We're greatly blessed,' an elderly man told me when I asked him about young people wanting to take to the streets. 'I thank God. Our king understands us and he's just raised the salaries of everyone, and we live in peace unlike other countries.'

Sometimes, I think part of the survival technique is to inhabit the limits that have been drawn for you. To convince yourself it's for the best. To silence any voice of doubt or rebellion and to start moving within those boundaries.

I was always convinced that, like me, everyone from my country/region wanted to leave. I was convinced that everyone had this restlessness about them, always looking for new frontiers. Of having that gnawing urge to escape because they're too scared of oppressive conformity. I've asked myself about friends and family who've stayed home. Some I now know are there by choice. They're with their families, they have jobs and kids and relatively secure lives.

I don't know when I developed the Need to Go. For a while, the notion of living like everyone else and doing what everyone did was appealing. Stability is extremely seductive. It still is sometimes, especially when I'm in a car or on a plane, rushing to a story that just broke, which I know next to nothing about and am expected to deliver an editorially sound brief about live on air in a few hours.

Or when I'm struggling for words to describe someone's suffering or to 'sum up' centuries of atrocities and oppression.

I often think, 'Someone somewhere is having a perfectly fine evening. They're at home with their family, cosy and content and here you are chasing! Always chasing, Shaimaa, and not really getting anywhere.'

*

When I went back to Alexandria for visits, my late uncle would always ask me, 'When are you coming back? I miss you all. This home is dead without you.' I never had anything to tell him. I wanted to say 'never' but that was too harsh for someone I loved so dearly.

He'd say, 'If it's a job you're after, find one here and come back.' To him and to so many friends and family, travelling was the variant to the desired state of being at home. I never understood that, hard as I tried.

To me it was the exact opposite – but also, and this was a very difficult realisation, there was no home for me. There was the notion of it: people, music, memories and food, which all traced back to Egypt. But in my heart, I have no permanent home. 'Home is where your family is,' my mum once told me. I was crying when we first moved to Doha – that I left all my school friends and my hometown to come to this strange place.

I know deep inside me that Egypt is a home of sorts, and that if any harm befalls it, the pain will be visceral. I know I feel pride when an Egyptian makes it in any field. I know nothing lifts my soul more than Egyptian humour, Egyptian food. And yet I know that nothing suffocates me more than Egyptian crowded streets where noises, nuisances and harassment attack you from every corner. Nothing crushes my spirit more than that Egyptian expectation of politeness and propriety and the utter, utter smallness and the Knowing of One's Place.

Naguib Mahfouz, the Egyptian novelist and Nobel Laureate, said, 'To be truly global you have to delve into what's truly local.' Martin Scorsese also said a similar thing. I realise now there's nothing truly local about me. I fear that in my endless quest to escape and to be a Citizen of The World, I'm of all places and not of any place.

What's painfully ironic is that I, of course, have been assigned titles when I moved to the all-coveted West: Egyptian. Arab. Muslim. Hijabi. Woman. Titles I carried and was expected to be the ambassador of, when needed.

And yet I know from my core that while some of each is true about me, none of them define me and oh, how so much easier life would have been if they did. When I talk about home and the experience of the Egyptian/Arab women, I talk about it from a safe and sometimes, I feel, fraudulent distance. But it's a distance I fought my whole life for.

I see all those lists of '10 Arab women journalists to look out for', '20 Arab writers you have to know', the '30 under 30 Arab whatevers' and I think, why am I not on that list? Do I even deserve to be? Many of my colleagues at the BBC World Service and BBC World TV go back to their homelands as heroes, as the 'our boy/girl' who made it at 'the Beeb'.

I go back to being the small person who wanted to run away. I go back and try to squeeze myself so tightly into that place that's been created for and assigned to me. The polite daughter, sister, wife of … who aims to please. I re-wire my brain into thinking of myself as belonging to the collective and not to myself. I try to remember why I missed a place that is full of life, yet drains the life out of me. I try to remember why I call this place home.

# 16.

# SHELLEY

In dreams and imagination, time isn't linear. I dream of my son and he's a toddler, or a nine-year-old, and I forget he's a young man. Your present self goes back through time and comforts my younger self and that heals something – to rewrite the past, re-imagine it. Likewise I imagine myself rushing back in time to find you when you were nine or ten, to tell you then, that one day you will be an incredible voice in the world – you will be a foreign correspondent and people will rely on you for making a space in the loud international incessant chatter, for their stories – and that you won't be arranged into a marriage, you'll marry someone you choose, and we'll have a friendship that is so elastic that even as we run, we'll be pulled together by a connection spanning continents and time zones, over decades.

I don't know if we'll ever stop running. I have felt homeless since I ran from South Africa. I may 'fit in' to new countries, but I have grown a shape that sits comfortably nowhere. I know you carry heavy things – I feel like being a woman for you means to have to push away so much more in every direction to be yourself, than it does for me. All the more power to you, that you have become such a voice – found a way to be you in a powerful way.

You are enough.
The gift of you in the world is
More than you can imagine
Your words are enough.
Your life experience is enough.
You will always be enough.
Worthy of everything

*

Paul and I arrived back in Doha with a tiny, red-faced baby. I was wearing tea-strainers under my bra because my nipples were cracked and bleeding and I'd had mastitis in one breast and then in the other and it was the only way I could keep any material off my broken skin. I was still bleeding. Paul, who had been a medic in a brutal war in Zimbabwe, took the stitches out from my third-degree tears. He said I looked like I'd been through a war.

We arrived in Doha in September heat, and the authorities would not let us in.

'Where is your baby's exit visa?' an official asked me gruffly.

'He went out in my stomach,' I said. 'When we left, I couldn't get a visa for a child who wasn't born yet.'

I was overwhelmed and in pain and close to tears.

Anything could have happened.

And then, a miracle.

'Dr Williams!'

A beaming young man in a thobe cut through the officials, spoke curtly to the man holding us up and grasped Paul's hand. 'Is this your baby, Dr Williams?'

'That's Tim,' Paul said. 'Three weeks old. We're having a bit of a problem here, since our son didn't have an exit visa.'

'No problem, no problem, at all,' the student said. 'Just come this way. Congratulations, by the way.'

He didn't look at me, just at the baby, and at Paul.

He took our passports and whisked us passed the grumpy officials and into an airport office. Our passports were stamped, written on and returned. He said we would need a medical for the baby, and he gave us the name of the doctor who would do it.

We were in awe of such kindness. Mahmoud was a student of Paul's doing his final year of English. He also worked for the department of immigration at the airport.

We arrived back in our humming, air-conditioned apartment overlooking Al Rayyan Road and the Corniche. It felt as sterile and lonely as the moon.

A few days later, a present arrived from Mahmoud. Baby clothes – small jeans and a shirt – and a red-and-white teddy bear.

When Paul saw Mahmoud again and thanked him, Mahmoud said, 'You're very welcome. I wanted to ask you something, Dr Williams. My sister, she's in your class on the women's side. She hasn't been doing so well in the English classes …'

This is how I came to understand what *wasta* meant. Someone does something for you, a favour, which indebts you to them, giving them power, or *wasta*. And so now it was time for a return favour – Paul's duty was to help Mahmoud's sister do well in English.

He promised to do this. To assist her in class. Give her extra help.

Just as I was allowed as a Western expat to teach on the men's side, Paul was allowed as a Western expat to teach on the women's side. While my teaching on the men's side was a daily act of defiance, Paul was loved by his women students. He was the literature professor, a safe, wise, kind and unthreatening guardian of the Classics. At the end of classes sometimes, he would return home with helium balloons and cards with 'I love you' and 'you are my everything'. The attention and appreciation lavished on him was entirely innocent and asexual, and was rivalled only by the attention lavished on me. I was gifted cards and bracelets and gold pendants on the women's side.

I came back to teaching when Tim was three-and-a-half weeks old.

I was seen as heroic by my students for having had a son.

Paul and I did teaching shifts. I pumped milk at 7 am and went to work and taught until noon. I rushed back home with bursting breasts. Sometimes I'd take off my bra in the elevator and milk myself because my breasts were so rock hard that Tim wouldn't be able to latch on when I came in through the front door – and tiny though he was, he seemed to sense me coming close. Every day I walked through that door in my milk-soaked blouse and pressed my baby to engorged and too-slow healing breasts.

*

He woke every two hours through the night. I could barely function. I sank into a dark place. Decades later, I have a sense of gritty injustice and retroactive envy, but also annoyance, when I see young Western mothers rushing off to their 'mummy and me' groups, or mother and baby yoga classes, carrying their expensive lattes in reusable bamboo cups.

I was isolated in Qatar. Post-partum depression wasn't available to me or anyone else I knew. It was not yet recognised as a legitimate and wide-reaching experience of mothers in the months after giving birth. Sometimes I thought of throwing myself out of the window – but I knew I would not do it, because I loved my baby more than my life.

Our neighbours were Iraqi. She had just had a baby too, and the baby's legs were put into splints. I couldn't speak Arabic and she couldn't speak English. But sometimes we met outside the front doors of our apartments, and in rudimentary sign language we connected, sharing information about sleep, feeding. Her husband introduced himself to us one day. He spoke English.

'My wife,' he said, 'she's also my cousin. This is why the baby has something wrong with her legs. But she will be okay. I had a girlfriend in America and with her I have a thirteen-year-old son. But my wife doesn't know this. For her, this is my only child.'

That was a lot of information. I tried not to feel burdened by knowing more about my Iraqi neighbour's husband than she would ever know.

I was going to have to learn to live a dichotomous life.

Teaching on the men's side:

'Mrs Shelley, you should not be here teaching. You should be home looking after your baby.'

'Mohammed, I would like to stay home with my baby, to tell you the truth. But the university won't let me. They say if I leave, Paul will need to leave too. So here we are, stuck with one another for another semester.'

Teaching on the women's side:

'Mrs Shelley, you are so clever to have a boy. Your husband must be happy with you.'

I understood in that one second, the young woman's position, which she assumed must be mine too: I was somehow responsible for the gender of my child – a boy gets more points than a girl; therefore, wives who produce sons are a more coveted commodity. 'Hend, it's complete chance you know, whether you have a boy or a girl. Nothing to do with being clever. My husband didn't care if we had a boy or a girl – we're just happy to have a healthy baby.'

'But all husbands want sons.'

Overflowing with guilt and milk, I wanted to cry. 'Do they?'

'Of course,' she said and smiled at my ignorance. 'They want a son – someone they can be proud of – a legacy.'

*

I had been hired to teach, but at least on the women's side of campus, I was getting a deep education myself. Unlike you, I couldn't inhabit the local culture in any way – but I was exposed in ways other expats weren't. I felt oversensitive to my young women students because I was in the aftermath of what I know in retrospect was birth trauma.

After Tim was born, I'd looked at Paul and said, 'I'm never, ever doing this again.' Of course, if someone asked me to go through the experience for Tim again, I would. But for another unknown person? Never.

And there were these young women, teenagers, going through the agony of childbirth, without their mothers, without a loving partner next to them, smacked and yelled at by their doctors. What right, I thought, do I ever have to complain? I felt, despite my struggles, spoiled – a fraud – someone who could come and go, who would never understand what it was like to be circumscribed by that reality. My love and admiration for these young women grew. My anger too.

And then, you're right. There was the poetry. The story of the desert.

One day, Ghalia came to me after class. She was in tears.

'Ghalia, what's happening?'

She shook her head. Couldn't speak.

'It's okay, you can tell me. When you're ready, okay?'

She held the sleeves of her abaya to her eyes, damped away the kohl that was leaving tear-stains down her cheeks. 'Mrs Shelley,' she said, 'I love poetry so much.'

'I'm so glad! Me too, Ghalia. That's wonderful! It's such a great form of expression. Have you been writing more poetry in the last few weeks?'

'I write so many poems. I have a book with all my poems and even for years I've been reading and also writing poetry. And these last weeks, I wrote more, after your class.'

'That's great,' I said. 'I love writing poetry too. I'd love to see your work if you want to share it.'

She shook her head and sobbed. 'My brother,' she said. 'My little brother. He turned eighteen. Now he has told me that he forbids me to write any more poetry. That I must destroy my books and all my poems. That no decent Qatari girl should be ever seen writing poetry.'

'What?'

She covered her face with her abaya.

I felt physically sick. It took me a stunned moment to comprehend what she was saying. 'Do you want to leave your book with me? I'll look after it. You can write your poems and give them to me. I'll keep them safe – I promise you.'

She looked up at me with her tear-filled, dark-ringed eyes. 'Mrs Shelley, you don't understand. My brother has *forbidden* it. I can't. I can't. I try to write the poems in my head. To remember them. But I can't. They're slipping away.'

She cried again, into her sleeve. I put a shaking arm around her shoulders. I felt cold.

Until then, the stories had upset me. But at that moment, I watched this young woman lose her voice – I saw her break and I had no words to give her. If someone stopped my words, I would want to die.

The door swung open. Students for the next class began to swarm in. She dried her eyes quickly, pulled her scarf more closely around her face. 'Sorry for the bother,' she said. 'Thanks for listening. Goodbye, Mrs Shelley.'

I was there as a young woman's voice dissolved into silence in front of me. And there was nothing to be done.

# 17.

# SHAIMAA

The pain you describe is so raw and real and left me angry on your behalf. I had no idea this was going on. I'm regretting every moment I saw you back then and didn't give you a big hug and tell you what a trooper you were and that you were doing so well given the impossible circumstances.

I lived through this with my sister when her youngest was born and we'd found out he had a heart condition. She was exhausted, fearful, sad, and she tried to hide it all. She tried, as she was conditioned, to get on with it and be practical – take the baby to hospital appointments, wake up every two hours to feed him, FaceTime her other two children (who were in a different country with their father) and smile and wish them a happy first day of school. I'm always in awe of my sister's strength. Never more than at this moment.

*

I still don't know how mothers do it. How they/you get up after your body has been so violently pulled, wrenched and slashed open. To have a tiny human to take care of when you can barely take care of yourself – to nurse a child, your bleeding breasts and your wounds all at once. To do it on next to no sleep or support and to then go out and face the world and be expected to function.

I know I'd never ever want to go through this. Seeing what my sister had to endure and hearing about your story makes that notion so clear to me. I never want to have a child.

This is actually the first time I've been able to write it down in black and white like that. For the longest time I haven't dared to think it. After my second unsuccessful round of IVF, I'd mustered enough courage to tell myself and then my husband that I didn't want children. I still can't say that to my family or his.

I'm in awe of you, my sister, and every mother who's expected to feel love, connection and the need to nurture while feeling completely alone in her physical and mental agony.

And you have a supportive partner! Someone who took out your stitches, who held the baby while you went to the bathroom, or took a shower, or maybe needed to cry. How many of your female students in Doha would've had that?

\*

Some of my Qatari classmates would come to university soon after giving birth looking so withered, barely focusing, with dark circles under their eyes. I remember thinking – how? How are you even focusing on Melville or Thoreau or goddamn linguistics when you have a baby at home?

I have no idea how you were able to teach – especially those men. With them telling you to go and take care of your baby, like you'd rather spend the day with them!

How many women have been denied permission to feel pain? To feel anger? Been told to suffer in silence because otherwise it'd be shameful and too much and that's not what women from good families do.

Those women who wait and hope for a baby boy to be worthy of their husband's love and for a secure place in their own marriage.

Those women in hospital rooms giving birth all alone – being yelled at by doctors while their husbands are at work or hanging out with friends until the whole thing is done.

The women who get abused in their own homes, on the streets, who get touched and grabbed and harassed and are supposed to take it on the chin and move on with their days.

When were women taught silence? I remember very well growing up that I was always told to keep my voice down. That good girls are not loud. Was that the beginning of my silencing? The irony of course is that in choosing broadcasting as a job, it required my voice as the major instrument.

We're taught to keep not only our voices down, but also our pain down. Our anger down. The hope, I guess, is that we disappear under an unyielding current of propriety, steadiness and silence.

As a teenager, when my period started and I'd get horrible cramps and be visibly aching, my mother or my grandmother would be shocked that I was showing it. My mother would say: 'We know the reason, right? So, there's no need for all this. It's fine. It'll pass. It happens.'

Along with being taught the basics of why and how this happens, I was also taught to hide that this actually happens; along with being taught how to use a pad, I was taught how to wrap a dirty pad neatly into pieces of newspaper and bury it in the trash so that no one (my father) would know.

I had a really bad period at school one day and got so sick that I had to call my father to pick me up. 'I have my period. It hurts so much and I threw up at the nurse's office,' I said on the phone.

I hung up and turned around and the sub teacher and the nurse looked at me as if I'd told my father I had a miscarriage in class.

'Why did you tell your father that?' one of them asked, wide-eyed.

'Because, Miss. It's a bad period,' I said, still not sure what I'd done wrong.

'Yes, but you don't tell your FATHER that! Unbelievable! She told her dad!' said one.

The other nodded, saying, 'Gosh, we'd suffer for days and no one would know we had it.'

*

I once hid a bunch of dirty newspaper-wrapped pads in the bathroom so that I could throw them away all at once and my father found them. My mother looked at me with a mix of shock and rebuke. When we bought pads, the pharmacist (usually a man) would wrap the pack in newspaper and/or put it in an opaque black bag.

We carried our shame in different ways. Sometimes on our bodies that were changing and then assaulted, and we were led to believe it was all our fault – sometimes in our hearts that held so much angst and sometimes in opaque black plastic bags from the pharmacy.

Maybe I can work my way through time and speak to teenage me and tell her that her burgeoning self-loathing and body hatred was not abnormal – that it was a natural result of an upbringing and a society that teaches you to hide everything about yourself. That the time your physicality asserts itself and flourishes into womanhood is the exact same time you are taught to disappear and to be silent and small. That when your body prepares you for perpetual physical pain you learn how to hide pain in all its forms – especially emotional and mental.

Maybe I can travel through time and tell younger me that those breasts and thighs and butt were not freak protrusions of which I should be ashamed, that this was my body growing and doing what it should, that I shouldn't hide it and if I showed it, I shouldn't expect it to be violated.

Maybe then I and many of us could have found the words and the voice for our hurt and rage. Maybe we could have said, 'I'm entitled to be angry when harassed and to ache when my periods are bad. Or to want to scream and fall apart when another small human being is slicing through my vagina to start its life.'

But silence is an effective weapon. When you take away the voice, you take away the words. When you take away the words, you take away the story. And then a whole narrative and existence is written for you as a woman by a society that sees you as a creature of a certain function or creature of inconvenience — or most commonly a source of shame.

And then there are the direct assaults. Like forbidding someone to write poetry — to literally deny her the words. Like your student Ghalia, prohibited from writing poetry by her brother. I still think about her and think how criminal it is to sequester a person's words, their voice and self-expression because of your own insecurities. Very few things are more poisonous than stifled words. I wonder if they ever found a way out.

Historically the Arab peninsula has long celebrated poets. It's been said that the Qur'an is a linguistic miracle and part of the reason its language is so mesmerising is that it was sent to Prophet Mohammed's people — the most eloquent of tribes!

It's a big part of the culture in the Arab world, including the Gulf. Men in their Majlises would sit around and listen to poetry. And yet for women, words are off limits — creative expression through language is shameful.

I want to give Ghalia her words back and tell her to shout them out. When she told you 'I try to write poems in my head to remember them, but I can't. They're slipping away,' I could see her slowly disappearing with her words. Sinking into a black hole where she was told all her poems and her sense of self should go.

I wonder if she found a way to save her words. Because without words, how are we meant to understand our lives? How are we meant to make sense of what has happened to us? Without words we lose ownership of our own stories and then we truly disappear.

# 18.

# SHELLEY

A Saturday in Doha. I called you in the morning at your
home.

'Would you like to join us at the Sheraton for a few hours?'

'Sure! Sure!'

I was relieved. I didn't know whether you'd even be able to
accept.

The Sheraton Beach Club was a slice of Western life with
some exceptions, superimposed on the Arabian Peninsula. At the
north end of the Corniche, the massive, pyramid-shaped hotel
raised its pointy head into the muggy air. We could barely afford
the membership, but it was not a choice now that we had a baby.
There was nowhere else in the country where I could find grass,
nowhere in the heat-stricken landscape where I could walk in
shorts, much less swim.

We parked in the car park and walked through the heat into
the air-conditioned foyer where a piano man dressed in a suit
played a white piano. Tim stared at the man's fingers running
up and down the keys. A massive glass elevator went up on the
inside of the pyramid, and we rode it just for fun.

We met you in that foyer.

You arrived and we hugged, and then we went outside. You, me, the baby, Paul. We were family.

The large pool was especially cooled to 30 degrees. Beyond the pool and the hot tub, the blue Arabian Gulf stretched out into the haze. Paul took Tim to sit on the grass.

You and I walked past the lonely parrot in the cage near the playground to the changerooms. We emerged changed. Young women ready for a swim. We would've fitted in anywhere. We might have been anywhere.

We slipped into the cool water and went for a swim. It felt so illicit. So absurd that walking around in a one-piece felt about as daring as running naked through Hampstead Heath might.

I was so happy to have you around.

It felt so normal.

But then, out of the corner of my eye, I watched three Gulf Arab men in white dishdashas sweep like apparitions around the pool. They looked at us with derision, or was it disapproval, hatred? It certainly wasn't desire. What were they doing here anyway?

I ducked under and swam to the other side.

I hoisted myself out of the pool. I was wearing a turquoise one-piece. I had the biggest boobs I'd ever had because I was breastfeeding. I felt one man's eyes on me – and if his gaze were fire, I would have been incinerated. But this was my territory. I was allied. I held my ground. The only place in Qatar where I could just walk around in the heat without being dressed from neck to ankle – and I wasn't going to have my day ruined.

He watched me as I walked to Paul and Tim. I picked up my baby and kissed him and held him to me, and I felt the disbelief of the man with his burning gaze. Up yours, I thought.

I sat with you on the rare green cultivated grass and we played with Tim. Paul went for a swim. The man in white floated away once he saw me with Paul and Tim, to find other more interesting viewings. I assume he thought you were my sister.

The few hundred square metres of grass and pools and semi-normality made me ache for Tim's sake, for a garden, for birds that sang, but mostly for trees and flowers and breaths of wind that didn't feel like they'd been forged in some heaving furnace.

Some days after, Paul said, 'Abdullah, our student, said he'd like to come over to cook us dinner to say thank you for everything I've taught him.'

'What? Come to us to make us dinner at our house?'

'Yes, he says he'll bring everything.'

'That feels weird.'

'Why? Shaimaa comes over. She's your student.'

'I know, but that's different. Abdullah's a stranger.'

'It'll be fine. Let's see what happens.'

'Okay. As long as I get to escape with Tim if it isn't working out.'

We waited from 6 pm on the designated evening. When he didn't show up by nine, we eventually got ready for bed. At ten there was a loud knock on the door. Abdullah came in. He went with Paul into the kitchen. I followed. He brought a bag of fresh vegetables, and handed me another, heavier plastic bag. It was warm. I looked inside and my stomach clenched. I thought I might be sick. I was holding the body of a warm chicken. Newly dead. Covered in feathers and blood. 'Fresh,' he told me, and took the plastic bag, placing it on the kitchen counter.

I walked out of the kitchen and overheard him say to Paul: 'I am sorry to say, Dr William, but I must say it — that I am offended that your wife — her hair is not covered.'

Paul laughed, surprised, I think. 'Why, Abdullah? It's just hair,' he pointed out. 'Also, with all due respect, you don't have to be here if you don't want to.'

Abdullah apologised. He hadn't realised he was out of line.

But I realised I'd heard enough. I was sleep-deprived as it was and Tim had just been put to sleep. Like millions of women in the surrounding countries, I retreated that evening from male company. I felt meaningless, invisible, as unnecessary as I'd ever felt. I also didn't care. I left the men to their chicken and went to bed.

In the morning I said to Paul, 'Okay, please, never again. That sucked. I know I have to deal with it outside every waking minute I'm away from this apartment, but you can't bring that oppression in here.'

'I'm sorry. I didn't mean it to be so bad.'

'You couldn't have known – but now we get it.'

Becoming acculturated was unavoidable, to some degree. My days as a young mother in the Arabian desert felt increasingly endless and pointless.

It was so hot in the summer, the temperatures sometimes hit 57 degrees. Paul took Tim out at five in the morning. They watched the rubbish trucks collecting the bins. They looked at the orange desert light until it was too hot and bright to bear. They followed stray kittens around the back of Dafna apartments.

I remained inside. There was no reason to be out. It just added stress and tension. Paul said, 'I hate how men call out and harass you wherever we walk.'

'No kidding. Me too.'

'So maybe just stay in.'

Wow. Seriously?

This was how it happened. It was too much effort to be out there, confronting the Big Bad Patriarch. I understood for completely practical reasons why a woman would elect to cover herself from head to toe. I understood it for the first time as liberating. If I were covered, I would have been left alone. It would have been the equivalent of an armour-plated vehicle in a warzone. And I wanted one.

I became like my Iraqi neighbour. Isolated. Depressed. I envied the expats in their compounds living in small versions of Britain and America with their own doctors and swimming pools in *Al Jazzi*, which was apparently so glamorous that the wife of one of the English professors who'd come from America and bribed their way into that compound cooed, 'When we got there, I thought I'd died and gone to heaven.' Well, good for her, I thought. Meanwhile, I went to the shops, to the university, to the Corniche (only with Paul to the Corniche), and stayed at home, weary. You've helped me understand now: I was being made to feel shame. I had no protective compound, no imported Western life. I was a sitting duck. I didn't feel shame, though. I just felt tired.

\*

Doha, Qatar was a crucible in which our lives converged. I felt confronted at every level after I returned with my baby. I began to wonder how I would ever find myself again.

One day Paul and Tim and I received an invitation from you and your mum.

We came to visit you.

We met your mum, and your sister.

I think they loved meeting Tim.

I remember your big room. The posters on the wall. Your teenage self sitting on your bed while your mum cooked dinner and chatted to Paul.

I felt like you and I were the kids.

I look back on the photos of you we took in Doha that day.

You were nineteen. You were so beautiful. To think that this young person thought her body was a compilation of

107

'freak protrusions' – to imagine you being assaulted, learning to be ashamed ... I just can't bear this. It's a crime against your humanity, your childhood, your right to be you. And maybe then I had an inkling, but I didn't know the details – and if I could've, I would have told you and will now join the older you to tell the younger you: you are precious; don't doubt yourself, your body, your validity; don't doubt your voice.

Your voice.

You found your voice!

I knew you when not many people heard you expressing yourself in English.

And then suddenly, there you were, on QBS – a radio host.

How did your friends react? Your family?

It takes such courage to say you don't want children. Did any of those young women in your class have a choice? You and me, Shaimz – we were the lucky ones in that crucible. I got to say, after giving birth, 'I'm never doing this again.'

You got to say, 'I'm never doing this.'

The shaming of the female body – blaming it or praising it for producing, or not producing. How is that not insanity?

At my brother's bar mitzvah, the rabbi would not shake my hand or come too close, in case I was having my period – in case I was 'impure' – if he touched me, he would be impure too. I felt, then, like a contaminant – and this is how so-called culture and religion plays out in everyday life. Never mind that the root of this behaviour lies in the Jewish belief that when you're fully immersed in a physical event (menstruation, sex, birth, death), it pulls you away from the sacred into the intensity of that physical event and it takes an act of will (and prayer) to emerge from that, to 'purify'.

But what if you believe, as I do, that intense physicality is sacred in itself?

I refuse the polemic which makes women feel less-than, which leads to them being shut out, cut off. You're a more valuable person if you have a boy child, your body is a shameful thing that contaminates others ... regardless of the insights and wisdom found in our ancient holy books, if this results in the sense that having a period or being a person who has a period makes you someone to be avoided, shut out, blacked out ... then what value does it have?

Our religious and cultural inheritances are close relatives.

The Big Bad Patriarch. What is his fucking problem?

The Qur'an is a linguistic miracle.

The Talmud is a fount of deep wisdom.

Leave these texts in the hands of women for the next two thousand years and see what happens.

In the English department staffroom, that first year of being a mother, I met a bubbly Iranian woman, Reza. She had just arrived in Qatar with her two sons – and she lived in Dafna, a few apartments away from ours.

'Would you like to come to our house? I would love to make you some Iranian food,' she said. 'Let's not be lonely women when we're at home.'

'I'd love that,' I said.

I visited Reza in her apartment, which looked exactly like ours, except in mirror image. Persian carpets lined the entrance. Beautiful ornaments from a land unimagined adorned her dining room table. I brought Tim over, and her youngest son, Farhaz, who was eleven, sat on the floor and played with him, sweet, gentle, a devoted babysitter immediately.

Babak was fifteen. He skulked in and out of the living room looking at his mother with annoyance and at me with suspicion.

She waved him away with a laugh. 'Don't mind him,' she said. And then to me, with more seriousness. 'He's just like his father.'

While Farhaz shared toys with my crawling baby and lay on the generic pale green carpet that graced the floors of hundreds of Dafna apartments, I talked to Reza.

The beauty of female connection is that it can be easy to bond quickly. We all have our body narratives, and this quickly, in this case, led to soul narratives.

While Qatar was restrictive, while it seemed like a prison, it was also a place for runaways, a dichotomous entity. I finally had a job, a salary, a roof over my head, a place where I wasn't in fear of particular acts of violence I'd grown up being exposed to in South Africa. Your mother found a job, status and income, and you could go to university. And Reza, too, was an escapee, a runaway from Iran.

'I'm here, thank God, to get away from my husband's family,' she said. She looked quickly to see if Babak was anywhere around. 'He doesn't speak English much anyway,' she said. We went into the kitchen, where she took out the beautiful meal of saffron rice (she'd brought the saffron with her from Iran) – the special bit, she told me, was the burnt underneath of the rice. The more I loved her food, the more she shared with me. She said when she was first married, she cooked this rice, not to her husband's liking. Her in-laws were so incensed that she'd cooked their son a bad meal that they beat her.

'They beat me so hard and so long, Shelley, I soiled myself and passed out.'

I was almost sick.

We sat in the living room. No mention was made of the word 'abuse'.

'You're still married to him?'

'Yes, of course,' she said quietly. 'But I'm here in Qatar now. Teaching at the university.'

Farhaz looked up at me from where he lay on the floor showing Tim a toy train. A wide smile broke over his face like sunshine. 'I am a feminist,' he said, and caught his mother's eye. 'Not like my brother,' he said.

'No, he's not like his brother. Babak speaks little English. Farhaz speaks English, Farsi and Arabic. He's been here three weeks and already his English is almost as good as mine,' she said. 'One day maybe he'll work for the United Nations.'

# 19.

# SHAIMAA

My mum wasn't crazy about the idea of me working in QBS. She would've much rather I'd found an internship or a training position at a bank or better still at university. She was happy when I eventually ended up teaching English after I graduated while keeping my QBS job.

At first, though, I sold it to her as a summer job where I could make use of my time and make some money, I also promised I'd take an extra summer course at uni, which meant I'd graduate early. She liked the sound of that. She certainly did not like the music I played. She rarely ever listened to me. But I knew she was pleased that I was pursuing financial independence.

My friends thought it was really cool I got to be a radio DJ. It's not a job many women get to do, and in Doha of all places. I also played hip-hop, which wasn't to everyone's liking! I got a lot of grief from the station manager who would get a lot of complaints about my choice of music.

'Some of the songs are unacceptable. The ones about women's body parts. You know what I mean. Please be careful,' he said to me once.

The other time I got in trouble was during Christmas, when I did an hour of holiday songs. 'This is a Muslim country. Change the music now,' he shouted on the phone.

So I played Snoop Dogg's 'Gin and Juice'. No Christmas references.

I remember going to uni and my friends handing me requests for my next show and I'd feel so happy, especially when I got to spend hours in the music library at the station in the 'banned' section, for music with explicit lyrics that we were barred from playing on air. Hip-hop filled most of those shelves. The racy covers were of course obscured in aggressive black marker.

I learned a lot, made many mistakes, put up with a lot of lewd and condescending remarks from both expat and Qatari colleagues – because women in the media are 'game' as I began to learn, especially young, single women in the media.

Despite all that, I was making my own money and I had slowly begun to find my voice. Literally!

I do hope Farhaz has made it to the UN. I hope he treats his partner better than his mother has been treated by hers …

I *live* for the burnt bottom of the rice! This was always my special bit. It had to be the right type of crunch. Not too burnt – golden and beautiful having absorbed all the good fat and left with the heat long enough to sizzle and fry. When my mum made rice, she'd say, 'there's "Mehar-mesh" for you!' meaning the crunchy bit.

Someone once told me that in Egyptian culture this was a sign that a woman couldn't perfect her rice. That she burnt the bottom and was about to ruin it. I should've known then that so much of what 'culture' decided was bad was going to become one of my favourite things.

Whenever I saw a photo of what looked like a cake which turned out to be tahdig – Iranian rice with the burned side flipped on top and decorated with dried pomegranate, my heart fluttered.

I knew then that this was a cuisine and culture after my own heart. The sectarian (Sunni–Shia) rivalry and the Saudi Arabia–Iran proxy conflict across the region, as well as Iran's nuclear ambitions have made it almost impossible to explore or visit. Professionally and personally Iran still fascinates me. The music, the art and of course the food! There's so much to know. And while the geopolitical narrative dominates, it's the people's stories that always grip me.

Many have risked their lives taking to streets rejecting their government's oppression in the name of religion. Many are in prisons or have died calling for freedom and accountability. Many others, including fellow journalists, detained or harassed for doing their jobs.

*

Everything Iranian fascinated me from politics to silk rugs to mixed grills. I have yet to meet an unattractive Iranian woman. As far as I'm concerned, Iranian and Afghan women are the epitome of beauty. Is it a coincidence that these two countries are among the most repressive for women? And that to be their full selves many women from both countries have to escape their homelands? There are so many facets and factors to this oppression of women.

Geography is everything. The borders within which you're born determine the big things. How free and safe you feel. How stable your life and your income will be. Whether you'll have an education or not. Whether healthcare is an option for you.

For women, it also determines the smaller things. Whether the hair showing from underneath your hijab can land you in jail. Whether encouraging other women to go to school can earn you a bullet in the head. Whether getting behind a wheel and saying that driving was a right for women as well as men would mean you being tortured in jail or forced to leave your country. Whether refusing to marry someone could see you sprayed with acid. Whether leaving your house would almost always guarantee sexual harassment.

Geography renders the small acts of driving, going to school or getting dressed in the morning 'everyday acts' for some and 'acts of life and death' for others.

You're right, Qatar was a place for runaways. It was a place where we ran away for better financial opportunities and if I'm honest it was my escape from the overpowering noise of my homeland.

My summer English teaching job was at a small ESL centre. The job was to teach a group of Iranian students who were nurses at the main hospital.

Men *and* women, if you can believe it. Two men and three or four women all together in one small classroom in the Doha summer heat with buzzing air conditioning. I'd sometimes rush from my radio job to get to class on time. The students were always pleasant, polite and funny.

We'd laugh about some of the examples in the ESL books. 'My name is Peter, I like to go dancing with my friends.' There were caricature-like pics of men and women dancing. The women would giggle and the men would say 'never!' and we'd all laugh – knowing what that would mean if it happened in public in their country. I've been told some private parties in Tehran, though, would be too wild for me to handle.

Looking back, I wish I'd kept in touch with them. I wonder where they are right now – still in Doha, or back in Iran – and whether they too recognised how devastating those divisions in our sects and politics were. All I know is that I really enjoyed their company and, of course, enjoyed hearing about Iranian food.

My visits to your Dafna apartment changed Doha for me. For the first time I had an escape. A place where I could say things and ask questions and not be seen as crazy or out of line. With you and Paul I could talk about my dreams out loud, of a different life, of adventures and travelling. Those dreams were valid and encouraged. Even if I was young and naïve, I felt heard and seen at your place. I was me. Not a young auxiliary of my parents. I'd never felt like that before among other adults.

I remember exactly how it came about. I was talking to you on the phone. You'd lent me a couple of your books, *To Have and to Hold* and *Freefalling*. That week I felt like I was floating!

*I know a writer!* I kept telling myself ... *A. Real. Life. Writer. I'm reading her books and I know her! The writer is my teacher!*

We were on the phone and I was telling you how wonderful your stories were and that I couldn't believe some of what happened in *Freefalling* actually happened to you. I must've said/ begged to see you for coffee or something, and you then kindly invited me to your place.

'Oh! You'd allow that?!' I said, trying to contain my excitement.

'Yes. I'd allow that,' you said with so much kindness.

\*

Being with you guys was a portal to a different kind of living. Where people wrote and swam freely and escaped violence and fell in love and travelled-not-with-their-parents. It was a place where I felt that things were possible, where people could *do* things. When I was in that apartment, I'd forget I was a young Middle Eastern woman. I was just a person. The heaviness of all the restrictions and expectations would just evaporate for the hours we were all together.

I saw the way you were with little Timmy! You talked to him like a person. It wasn't the usual baby talk I'd heard from other mothers before. Paul was there, he was involved. He carried him and sometimes would take him in the room to comfort him when he cried so we could hang out.

I could see you were exhausted and sometimes frustrated either with work or with Tim not eating or sleeping enough. Despite you growing more depressed and desperate to leave, you never stopped being kind to me. Being with you gave me hope – it gave me energy, and, in some way, you passed on a sliver of magic of what a creative life would look like.

What I also loved was that it seemed like you and Paul were struggling to understand the place. You! Our treasured, well-respected professors at Qatar University dared to drop the stiff formal facade and ask questions. You had no problem saying how odd or screwed up things felt to you. It seemed that despite your worldly experience we were both learning about Doha together and there were things I felt I could tell you about the culture. You were so open and real and unbothered with appearing any other way than who you were, and I just thought, wow! See, there are people like that! They exist!

\*

And then there was the other life changer: QBS. I couldn't have imagined the ways in which working in that small radio station would affect my life. Like our visits, working at the Qatar Broadcasting Service changed my relationship with Doha.

For the first time ever, I had a job. I was making money that I could put in the bank and withdraw when I needed it. I didn't have to ask my mother. QBS gave me my first taste of financial independence and in a way fed an urge that then became an addiction if you will: to work. To have a job.

And what a job! To be doing the thing I loved the most in the world. To be around music. To spend a day picking through rows and rows of CDs and just park up at the hip-hop section at the small QBS library and forget time.

I think I was in love with broadcasting for much longer than I realised. I used to pretend I was a presenter when I was a little kid where I looked at the wall, imagining it to be a camera, and read viewers' letters. My sister and I have a recording where we did an audio variety show. We sang and told bad jokes and the show ended with Mum walking into the room sharply telling us to 'turn that thing off and do your homework and chores'.

But QBS wasn't about broadcasting for me in the beginning. It was about being around all the music I'd loved for so long and had very limited access to. A university colleague who was a famous presenter and a star student had agreed to make an introduction to the boss after all my personal attempts failed.

I was training at first, observing some of the radio DJs for a couple of months and was then given a half-hour trial, then an hour, then a whole show. It felt like forever until I got on air.

I had no idea what I was doing – I was learning on the job, as I did it.

I remember messing up in my first half-hour. I can't remember how exactly, but I was trembling and on the verge of tears and then I got my first call from a listener who said I was doing a good job and it was nice to hear a new voice on QBS and that they hadn't heard nineties hip-hop on the radio for a while, and it was like someone had pumped me with adrenaline and oxygen.

I also distinctly remember that the day before my first time on air I got into a big accident with a huge trailer and wrecked my mum's car. So, I then had the stress of braving the Doha streets to get a taxi and being allowed through the check points of the TV building to catch my first few minutes on live radio.

I'm indebted to my time there so very deeply for so many reasons.

Not only did it afford me financial independence and allow me to play the music I loved, it also taught me how to use my voice – literally! It taught me how to have a relationship with the microphone and be aware of sound, of mixes, of jingles.

Of course, I was atrocious at the beginning (not sure I got much better by the end). I was/still am a fast speaker (mostly I'm afraid of ideas and thoughts running away). I had to do voice training and breathing exercises.

'They'll either love you or hate you. As long as they don't ignore you.' My trainer and mentor at QBS was a half-British, half-Jordanian man called Eddie. He reminded me so much of Dustin Hoffman. Eddie had this 'fed-up-with-everyone-been-there-done-that' air about him. When the manager of the station brought me to his office, he nearly rolled his eyes. ANOTHER ONE, I felt him say!

He took me to the studio, told me to sit behind the mic and the mixer and sat in the chair opposite, his eyes on me and said, 'Okay, do a show.' I was so nervous, I played a song, faded it quick and then said in a very unsure voice, 'That was … so and so …'

'What was that?' he interrupted. 'What's the singer's name?' he asked.

'Umm Mary J Blige,' I said.

'Well then say that! Why are you waffling? Don't try to sound like the others. You are not the others. Don't use unnecessary words to fill air. People want to listen to music not you.' He was harsh and brash and didn't give two fucks, but he taught me so much about the fundamentals of radio. Not that I applied all of his rules. I made so many stupid mistakes, filled the air with nonsense, blabbered till the cows came home and at times didn't take the job as seriously as I should have. But the radio studio became my home. The microphone was my companion and the music my way of telling the world that I existed. There were so many ups and downs in those seven years but I was slowly and sometimes painfully finding myself.

One of my most horrific moments was when I'd filled in to read the news one morning and made a lot of mistakes on air, mispronouncing words and names. When I walked into the next studio to say hi to the DJ after the news, he just looked at me and said, 'You know you're rubbish, right?' I was still smiling and didn't register what he was saying. 'Honestly that was so bad! You know people are listening to this laughing at you, right?'

All I could say was, 'Okay, how long have you been doing this?'

'Doing what?' he scorned.

'Being a DJ.'

'I'm NOT a DJ. I am a presenter,' he asserted.

'Well, I've only been doing this for a few weeks,' I said trying to hold back my tears.

'That's nobody's fault. You're not here to learn on air.'

I said thanks and walked out.

I don't know how I finished that shift or how I went back on air for the next bulletin knowing that he was looking at me through the glass and listening to me and picking on every single slip-up.

I went home and called a friend, and I don't think I said any words. I was just bawling on the phone.

The big 'full circle' moment of the story was that years later we'd meet again in a small studio. He was reading the news and I was the presenter of the BBC World Service's main breakfast news program. We looked at each other, smiled and said hi. My co-presenter asked if we knew each other. He said, 'Yes. Shaimaa and I go way back.'

'We worked at the same local radio station in Doha,' I said.

I'll never forget that day at the DJ studio, though. I felt broken and that listeners were laughing at me, like he said. It was my first brush with 'real world' callousness. Of course, I got a lot more criticism after that – people mocking my voice, my accent, my choice of music.

I'd learn both how to navigate the airwaves and the work environment. Both came with great difficulty.

It wasn't easy because I was trying to figure out who I was, who I wanted to be, with everyone judging my every move. What I wore, how I laughed, who I chatted with. If I talked with one of the technicians he'd think we were best friends and start asking me uncomfortable questions. If I laughed with another, he'd think we were dating.

I remember sitting with a colleague in an office wanting the ground to swallow me up as he started talking to me about his wild trips to Europe and the prostitutes he'd entertain and how drunk he'd get.

It was a strange place to work. It wasn't a regular workplace like a school or a bank. Misogyny and sexism were rife among both locals and expats.

It was the first place I'd learned what it meant to be a young woman in the world, outside the segregated walls of Qatar University. Working the media in Doha meant working in a male-dominated society. Not many women worked in the field. Certainly not many local women. Yet, for all its pitfalls, it was comparatively a much safer environment than other workplaces both in Qatar and Egypt.

As I was examining who I was at work, I was also learning that mini-harassments were a common daily occurrence. I saw myself change a lot and realised that these changes were in response to the agitations I'd been exposed to the day or week before. I became more closed off, more aggressive and suspicious. The minute I decided to act the way I wanted, to wear what I wanted, I paid for it in the form of an unwanted advance or inappropriate remark by a man at work.

*

A male presenter sat me down one day to talk about my potential as a sports reporter. The discussion quickly turned into an invitation for dinner at his place.

Another co-worker said he wanted to hang out and get a meal, only to then suggest that we 'have some sex'.

Then the time a male colleague commented on how tight my jeans were. It took every bit of strength and self restraint in me not to scream out and slap him. But this started years before that.

A life of harassment: subtle and often not so subtle.

It began after I turned ten.

It's around this time that everything got darker. My flesh stopped being my own and became an extension of my religion and my unforgiving society.

After ten, my body would start to change and so would my relationship with it and my ownership of it.

After ten, I would grow up and become less of my own and more of everyone else's: family, society and random men on the street. They all had a stake and a say in how the flesh and fat sat on my bones.

After ten I began to slowly realise and understand that being violated in any way was going to always, always start with an assumption that it was my fault.

And I learned the best way to get over it was to 'get over it'. To push it inside. To repress it in whichever way I knew how at the time. To laugh it away. Cry it away. But never ever confront how it affected me.

After ten, the Big Bad Patriarch really began to show himself. The cruellest irony is that the Big Bad Patriarch manifested himself through the women in my life. My mother, my grandmother, my aunts. They all absorbed the message the patriarchy carried, and injected it faithfully.

The main principal internalised from the Big Bad Patriarch was propriety. This was achieved by obedience, smallness and silence. It was hammered in constantly after ten. What 'good girls' should do and be. More accurately what 'good girls' *shouldn't* do or be.

It was soon after I turned eleven that I was sexually harassed for the first time. My initiation into the womanhood sorority.

I was at my grandma's house and my mum had agreed to let me, my cousin and her friend go out for a walk in the street nearby. It was a popular street in the area, full of shops and a couple of ice cream places which is what we were after.

It was a big day. Freedom with a taste of ice cream. I would finally be out on my own with a couple of other girls away from our parents' gazes and instructions.

Except of course my grandmother had a few words before we set foot outside. 'Stay together. Don't go too far and don't spend your money on stupid things.' I think she meant ice cream, and of course that was our plan!

This outing needed to go without a glitch. 'Okay, Shaimaa! Don't trip and fall,' I remember telling myself. 'Don't fight with your cousin or her friend. Hold on to the money! The last thing you want is to go back to Mum or Grandma and say you lost your money. That'd be a sure way of never going out on your own again.'

I was so excited, though. The street. All this stuff in it! All those people. The adventures. The shops.

What I wasn't seeing at this point were all the men and boys on the street, some of whom were lurking. Watching to see who they were going to torment next. The vultures waiting for their feed – us.

I was busy deciding which ice cream flavour I wanted. We were discussing that and hadn't realised we were being followed. It was Alexandria in the summer and the streets were always teeming with people. And this particular street was always busy.

So, when three boys started bumping into us in one of the bookshops where we were looking at comic books I didn't think anything of it at first. But then the same boys pushed into us again and again and when I turned around and showed that I saw them, that must have signalled that it was game on. That we were going to be their entertainment for the afternoon.

They started laughing and yelping within inches of our ears. And then one of them groped me. I'm not sure which one. They weren't much older than we were. All I remember was that touch. It was a touch unlike anything I'd ever felt before. No one had ever touched me like that. The entitlement and the aggression of it. It didn't hurt. It burnt. How could something so common as the act of touching become so violent in a split second?

I had no words for it. Except that I started trembling. With fear, with anger, with safety and innocence being snatched away from me so suddenly and so nonchalantly.

Is this what it feels like when a burglar has been in your house? One moment it's your home, the next it's a familiar place drenched in terror. Even when the burglar is gone the stench of the violation is still there.

It's like a pact had been broken. That thing that promised to contain you and keep you safe has been desecrated and you go from living in it to constantly trying to protect it from an expected threat.

I went out that day an excited child ready for the world's adventures. And in a few minutes, I was vomited out into adulthood – the bile of abuse all over me.

How did he know it was okay to do this to me, that boy? How did he develop this power and joy from it? Did I miss something? Was there a special lesson for boys about what to do with girls on the streets? When does it start? Do they teach this in school or at home? Does that happen to all girls?

'Home!' my cousin said. The three of us held hands and rushed back to my grandparents' house.

The boys were still behind. After the groping, the verbal harassment started. I knew words hurt.

But when a stranger talks about your body, how your trousers sit on your ass, the hair on your arms, your walk … it makes you want to shed your skin. It makes you want to walk out of your physical self and fly away. Nothing prepares you for that. For your body being used as a weapon against you.

No one tells you that this is going to accompany you for the rest of your life, this kind of shame.

The stench of violation.

In a few minutes I went from an excited child who was ready to explore her grandma's neighbourhood to an exposed female who wanted to disappear.

This was by no means the worst incident of harassment I'd faced. But it was the first and with it came shame and anger. I was robbed of a good day and a good ice cream.

I was also robbed of innocence. The street stopped being the place where I played with cousins and friends and bought candy. It became a place where people grabbed you and talked about your privates and then mocked your anguish.

'Kefaya! Enough!' I shouted at them on the verge of tears.

'Kefaya!' one of them said back mocking me and they all just burst into laughter.

'You talked to them?' my mother reprimanded when I told her what happened.

'That's what they want; if you engage and make a scene, they win. It's you who's humiliated not them! You. Don't. Say. Anything. You just keep your head down and keep going. Do you understand?' Mum said.

Say nothing.
Keep head down.
Keep going.

Say nothing.
Keep head down.
Keep going.

Say nothing.
Keep head down.
Keep going.

I kept repeating this in my head, with tears streaming down my cheeks.

*

My first lesson about sexual harassment. Silence. Smallness.

'Let me tell you something, Shaimaa. When something like this happens. When some boy is being an idiot (as in: when some boy sexually harasses you), they lose nothing. If you start making noise, you get labelled. You lose.

Lesson two. If you defend yourself, you lose.

'Were you loud? Were you laughing or smiling for no reason?' my grandma chimed in.

I tried to remember if I laughed. I probably did. I was having a good time until I got sexually harassed.

'And why are you wearing that shirt? Your arms are bare. It's too short. Your bottom is showing.' Not sure if this was my mum or my grandma.

Lesson three. It's my fault. I did something. I deserved this.

This day wasn't just the first day I was sexually harassed. It also was the first day I was doused in shame and robbed of the language to explain to myself and to others what happened to me. I was robbed of the words to describe it for what it was.

Silence doesn't only suppress what needs to be said. It also slowly erases what needs to be said from your core. So you have no words for your feelings. And if you have no words for them it's much, much easier for them to remain unsaid. And if they remain unsaid, it's much, much easier to render them invalid. Who's to say that these feelings are even real or worth feeling, let alone worthy of being talked about?

My friend and I were chatting about this. Asking why we, women in our forties, still find it difficult to explicitly tell someone to fuck off when they're hassling us.

'It's not that we don't know how to react. We just don't have the language to react. More precisely our language to react to harassment has been taken away from us when we were taught to stay silent in the face of any violation,' I told my friend.

We were taught that the only way to deal with it is to ignore it. But by ignoring it we've also ignored our own feelings. We've denied ourselves the right to be angry and hurt. We've forbidden ourselves from understanding what effect this has had on us over the years. And instead of that anger and hurt being directed at the person who deserved it, we keep it inside of us – festering, malignant.

It wasn't even the culprits who were telling me to be silent. They were safe in the fact that we were going to be taught it.

Maybe not that day when I yelled at that boy, but eventually it was going to happen. I was going to absorb that radioactive notion of shame and mute anger.

All my life I wanted the freedom to do things on my own – to walk the streets and get myself from A to B with no parental supervision. Here I was at eleven – confronted with the reality of what that meant. That with the freedom to be in the streets came the aggression of the streets. That by being on the streets

I'd involuntarily chosen to be on the losing side of an every-day conflict.

My body was no longer the vehicle through which I floated in the sea, fell out of trees or ran fast in a game of hide-and-seek on the street. It was now the carrier of my family's honour and of my potential sin and their shame. A moving target.

The heaviness came in repressed emotions. Everything had to be contained tightly lest it invite unwanted attention. My happiness, my sadness. Laughter and tears were both to be tucked away quietly like my body. 'Stop being so loud!' was my marching order from almost all the adults in my life as I went through my teens.

It has altered my neural pathways in many ways, this quashing of being. It affects everything: the way you slowly and steadily deny yourself the right to be you in what you wear and what you do and the way you are in the world.

The restrictions define you and your fight to liberate yourself also means the risk of feeling absolutely lost without them.

This presented itself most here in Sydney, when I realised that the things I loved the most, like swimming, hanging out on the beach, were also the things I'd feared the most – the action of indulging in a good time and doing so wearing what I wanted when I wanted.

I gave myself heatstroke one weekend spending the day on the beach and being in the sun for so long. I loved it! I was in a bathing suit almost the whole day and wore a sleeveless T-shirt and a pair of shorts to go home.

It was like there was a small faint voice going – this is *you* doing this. This is you wearing this T-shirt and shorts – this is you enjoying yourself on the beach. Just you, not despite or because of anyone or anything else.

By the end of the day another voice seeped in, the self-erasing voice, the 'who-the-hell-do-you-think-you-are' voice, the 'you-know-you're-going-to-get-punished-for-that' voice.

I woke up the next day with a foreboding sense of guilt. I was truly waiting to be punished for what I'd done. For the fun I had and the skin I exposed. For the self I embraced.

It's a unique kind of oppression when you're turned against yourself. When it has been imprinted in your DNA that your body is not your own. The way this doctrine controls you even when those doing the controlling are no longer there.

You know the Big Bad Patriarch has done his job when he gets you to do it for him and watches your internal struggle, going through life fighting to understand your loss.

I have an unreasonable amount of envy of girls who can just put something on and go about their days.

The ease by which so many women especially in the West and in certain privileged classes of the Middle East approach clothing fills me with longing and jealousy. It's a loss that is both aesthetic and visceral.

*

Repression came in many forms, none more urgent and panicked than the repression of sexuality. A lot of that was and still is attached to women's clothing.

Getting dressed became an armour, a way for us to hide our bodies and confirm our chastity – God forbid any of us would want to look good or attractive. You can argue part of that is religion, yes. But a huge part of that mandate on what women should or shouldn't wear – what's acceptable and what's not – is cultural.

Across many conservative cultures and religions sex out of wedlock is forbidden. It is maligned and vilified. It was almost always attached to violence. Sex was an attack. It was the source of all evil and disgrace. And the source of that was women. They, for some reason, were the instigators. Because why would a man assault a woman if she hadn't invited it? And the way a woman dressed was a key part of that alleged 'invitation'. 'Look how she's dressed,' has been an almost immediate comment I'd hear when a woman would complain about being harassed. It depresses and fascinates me that this is a conversation that's being had the world over including the West now.

Men, young and old, seemed to have agreed that women going about their day were target practice. I was groped, poked, touched, verbally and physically violated from that ill-fated age of eleven.

This became part of daily life in Egypt – like the country's unbearable traffic. It was something for women to endure, not for society to change, although in the last few years there seems to have been an awakening – a movement by women after so many tragic incidents in Egypt that they could no longer tolerate this. So many young women are becoming much more vocal. Again, not just in Egypt or the Middle East. I'm amazed by the courage and eloquence of young women speaking around the world. When I was growing up, though, that wasn't an option.

We had to live our lives knowing that whatever happened to us was our responsibility and ultimately our fault. We were both victims and culprits.

When you stepped out onto Egyptian streets, you took your body, your dignity and sometimes your life into your own hands.

A piece of clothing carried so much weight. It carried the judgement of society and the wrath of religion. Both were there to control us. Both did.

*

In my work in conflict zones people often told me about the effect of long-term war on everyday life. In Iraq, Yemen, Afghanistan and parts of Pakistan, I heard the same thing many times. You leave home and you don't know whether or not you'll come back. And if you do come back, you don't know if you'll do it in one piece.

'But you can't let that stop you,' a young man told me in Kabul after a bombing near the American embassy compound a few years ago.

Something about that was so familiar to me. Not that I'd experienced any proximity to physical danger and the life-and-death situations that war forces on every minute of one's life in a war zone. It was more about the life and death of the soul and sense of self. To me, braving the streets of Egypt as a woman, you really didn't know whether you'd come back with your spirit in one piece.

I think that's why I'm good at disappearing. The key to getting by was to not exist while getting by. The larger my size became, the more I learned to make myself small. To look at the ground, blend with my surroundings, willingly turn off my aura or magnetic field. It worked at times.

But it left so many scars. I'm forty-something now and I still have to remind myself to stand straight and look ahead while I walk. I catch myself smiling on the street as I enjoy music in my ear and I actively stop.

These experiences chewed you up and spat you back into the confinement of your home. It's very strange and heroic that millions and millions of women keep doing it.

The alternative, however, was to not be in the world. The alternative was to remain cooped up in our safe and stifling spaces. The sad thing about Egyptian streets is that with their viciousness also comes their vibrancy. There is so much to see and do, so much life happens on the streets but it seemed to only be reserved for the men.

'The streets are for the boys. That's where they learn about life. Girls learn that at school and at home.' One of Mum's lines that is etched with rage in my memory.

*

I have lately glimpsed a few traces of the self I've longed to be. A self who loves the sea, who wants to be in the water. A self that prays five times a day, reads Qur'an and can walk around in a swimsuit and a sleeveless T-shirt. A self that occupies this incongruity … embraces it. A self that is not yet strong enough to let go of the guilt and shame but that at least now knows they're there because this was done to her and that her life's work is the undoing of it all.

It's fascinating that you too used a war metaphor when talking about covering up on the streets. 'Like an armoured vehicle in a warzone,' you said.

Except this weapon finds its way through the toughest of armours and gets right to your core and makes you feel vulnerable and exposed again.

This was my armour: aka, my-mother's-rules-for-being-on-the-street-while-female:

- Don't smile while walking. Frown preferably.
- Look down. Keep head down.
- Walk fast. Don't linger.
- Wear long shirts that cover your butt.
- Do not bring attention to yourself in any way.

In a way, these rules worked. They made me good at disappearing and blending in with the background. They had a huge influence on my self-image. I've also developed a natural scowl now – it's just there all the time. I have to make an effort for it to straighten up. That's what years of frowning in public space can do to you. A scowl both on the inside and outside.

If I was inappropriately touched, a million questions would go through my mind. But it was always focused on me.

Did I:

Smile while walking?
Walk too slow?
Linger on the street?
Show too much skin?

You'd think that the more you covered the safer you were – but it really didn't matter. Women with bare heads, headscarves, even women who wore the niqab, where you could only see the eyes, have all been harassed.

*

When I tell people I love fashion, I always sense a dismissive chuckle. You wouldn't know it looking at me. I'm always in frumpy clothes – mostly shapeless with the sole purpose of hiding my breasts and my impossibly big and disproportionate bottom.

Hiding these offensive bulges in Egypt was a bid to try and deny any potential violator using what I was wearing as an excuse to harass me, although that never stopped them.

Yet I could spend hours looking at how some women dressed. How they combined pieces and looked so well put-together. How their arms and legs fit into smaller clothes. How nothing bulged out. How some women were free to express themselves through fashion and clothes rather than using clothes to hide themselves.

I laugh sometimes when I hear the term 'street style' – I think, 'What streets are they talking about?' Egyptian streets would crucify any woman who dared to look different. Egypt has perfected the lethal combination of harassment, ridicule and humiliation to a tee.

This would become a part of mine and my friends' lives. Our collective daily experiences went from verbal harassment, to inappropriate touching, to groping, to trying to rip clothes off, to regular abuse.

The attackers were random men or boys on the streets, shopkeepers, doormen, teachers, co-workers, even family members – sometimes more than one of those on more than one occasion in one day …

Eventually the people who taught us to be silent about violation were now the people we kept all of this from. We had to balance aggression on the streets and restrictions in our households.

If they knew what we went through on a daily basis, our mostly conservative families would react in two ways: 1. Blame us. 2. Restrict our movements even further to keep us safe. As opposed to, I don't know, have our backs and equip us with the strength we needed to brave the streets.

In 2013 a UN women's report said that 99 per cent of those surveyed were sexually harassed. 'That one per cent must've been at home that day,' I joked to myself when I read that.

Things have moved on quite a bit since I was eleven. Young women are now much more vocal. There's been a recent social media campaign encouraging women to speak up.

Activists, famous media personalities and even religious figures encouraged the girls to come forward and to not be afraid to tell their stories.

Yet all of this hasn't stopped the attackers. It will take time. It will take the changing of 'My-mother's-rules-for-being-on-the-street-while-female …'

It'll take many, many cycle-breakers to rid us all of the radiation of shame and silence.

*

Sometimes I think I'm a coward. I've run away. And will probably spend my life running away. But then I think maybe that was my way of self-preservation. And only by running away can I begin to think of a language to understand it all.

I don't live in Egypt now, but when I go home, I can feel my body growing tense. I armour up. I play scenarios in my head of what I would do or say if someone harasses me. Will it be physical or verbal? How would they touch me? What if it's boys young enough to be my sons? Mostly I'm disappointed in myself in advance because I know that my reflex is going to be that I keep my head down and ignore it.

There are now laws to criminalise sexual harassment. If only there were laws to criminalise the silencing.

When we work our way through time to my twelve-year-old self, please remind me to tell her this: 'You look fine. What you're wearing is fine. Laugh. Be loud. And if some horrible person harasses you, shout! Make a scene and stand up for yourself! Remember: it is NOT your fault!'

# 20.

# SHELLEY

It breaks my heart to think of your life from age ten onwards – how you had to learn to 'balance aggression on the streets and restrictions in your households'. I would tell the younger you that your body is yours, and yours alone. That you have a right to fight back if you're threatened, occupy space and be free to love yourself and to know that your voice is valid. That no part of you, no atom, is anything to be ashamed of.

But I'm older and, like you, I'm not naïve.

I know that this world, and the continent we were born on, is predatory and rabidly patriarchal.

Despite the #MeToo wave, billions of girls have no such hashtag luxury.

I use the word 'luxury' in an ironic sense.

It doesn't, anyway, stop the attackers.

The only way to stop them is to raise boys like Farhaz – who would more likely be out of the reach of the Big Bad Patriarch.

When you started coming over to our apartment in Qatar it was a reprieve for me. From the beginning, you were like a sister. I was twenty-eight and you were eighteen. You felt familiar. To you, it didn't seem to matter if my breasts were leaking milk all over my T-shirt, or if I was tired, if my hair was messy and I hadn't put away Tim's thousands of toy cars. You were my illuminator. Though Qatar was foreign to you, you had more street cred than I ever would.

Did we have a conversation once that went something like this?

Me: This guy followed me home from the university – I'm sick of being followed. Why does this keep happening?

You: Were you using your turn signals?

Me: Of course!

You: See, that's the problem!

Me: Why?

You: If you're signalling, it means, 'Follow me this way, follow me that way!'

Me: What?

You: Yep.

Me: That's not what they're designed for.

You: But that's how they're used here.

So, I stopped using my turn signals. Just swung out or into the roads as needed. And I stopped getting followed home. A miracle.

Road signs, indicators, car horns, all of those were used in different ways in Qatar as opposed to, say, London, or the USA.

Rules for Driving in Doha at Any Time:

- The biggest, most expensive car always has right of way.
- Speed up at a yield sign and hope for the best. If you slow down, you will be rear-ended.
- Don't use turn signals unless you want to be followed.
- Women driving cars present a special kind of novelty for some other drivers. Watch your back.

Similar to Rules for Driving in South Africa:

- If the light turns red, slow down for a moment only, and once you can see your way clear, speed through.
- Stopping could cost you your life. Stay on the correct side of the road when necessary.
- If you get annoyed, or feel like you're getting hemmed in, this could be a ploy to hijack you – so use the other side unless there is oncoming traffic that poses an immediate threat.
- An orange light is an incentive to flat foot it.
- Never break down. If you leave your car, every portion of it will be stolen by waiting car piranhas. (If you are rich enough to have a car, you are rich enough to be hijacked or robbed.) If you stay with your car, you are at a high risk of rape/assault/murder – and your car will be stolen anyway.

Once some genius in South Africa invented a device that shot flames out of the bottom of the car at the press of a button if the driver felt herself to be in danger. This deterrent was deemed illegal and unethical and banned from being developed or used.

This is why, though it may be hard for people to understand, Qatar felt to some degree, like a place to catch my breath. For a while.

Until icy fingers wrapped around my heart and began to crush the breath out of me.

You were my Decoder-of-Daily-Life-in-the-Desert. You, who walked in two worlds. This is why you are such a special reporter now. You can land in a brand-new country, like Australia, and before you even get over jet lag, you're heading to New Zealand to report on a volcano erupting in a once-in-a-life-time tragedy; or walking through the devastated fire-hit landscape listening to people, carrying their tears; or speaking about Aboriginal deaths in custody and rates of incarceration. And you detect and reveal an understory. I am in awe of that – of your passion for authenticity, your sensitive handling of people's heart stories.

*

I was the Jewish girl in Germany with generations of trauma mapped into her DNA – scrubbing floors for a crazy German lady who told me she hated me; I am the daughter of a man arrested by right-wing policemen who wanted to 'teach these Jews a lesson'.

I became, in Qatar, something else: I saw myself for the first time as 'other,' tied by blood and history to the people responsible for shooting my student Bassel when he was a thirteen-year-old boy trying to get medicines to his dying mother.

Hate is a waste. A friend of my grandmother's who survived the Holocaust said, 'Hate poisons only the hater.'

I worked in a strict Muslim country. I saw in Bassel, the same dark eyes of my younger brother.

I met you, a young Muslim girl ... and from the moment we connected, you were family. We were born on the same continent – *mud sisters* – coming out of the same earth; mud that is stronger than political geography.

If you go back far enough, we are closely connected by blood and heritage. Harry Ostrer, a doctor and Director of the Human Genetics Program at New York University School of Medicine (so, a respectable geneticist), says that you and I have common ancestors that go back four thousand years.

'Jews and Arabs are all really children of Abraham,' he writes.

We have unique genetic markers that bind us for hundreds of generations.

We go to war with our own mirror images – and we destroy ourselves.

I'm wary of telling a story that reinforces the myths of our times. I'm also wary of trying to create a story that is 'balanced'. The world is not balanced. Our experiences of it are not balanced. As long as a human being is telling a story, it will be filled with bias, and a unique making-sense-of-moments.

\*

#MeToo. I've buried this for years. It was so subtle it might never have happened. This is not the story of someone being taken at knifepoint and gang-raped, as a close friend of mine once was – but thirty years later, I am haunted by an event so brief it could almost have been imagined. But the residue does not go away. We were young, inexperienced – I more than he – as we lay naked together. The party had been at his house and I'd stayed over and we hadn't 'done' anything yet. Downstairs in the living room music pulsed from a stereo. Upstairs in his room, rain hammered down on the roof, ran rivulets down the window. I was in love with him. Or so I thought. Spring thunder spread across the sky, west to east – an ozone-rich Highveld storm. I was intoxicated with him. Ecstatic. Then he rolled onto me.

I didn't even register what was happening it, was so quick. He pushed himself into me. It lasted maybe ten seconds before I wriggled out from under him, shoving him off me. 'Stop it! What are you doing?'

'I thought it was better if it happens, you know, not all at once!' He was defensive, upset.

'You agreed we'd wait. I wanted to wait. You knew that!'

'We gotta start somewhere sometime,' he said.

I was miserable with guilt and a sense of having lost something.

I felt unreasonable. I'd obviously planned to sleep with him. Just not right yet.

It's difficult to recognise what they are, but they build, these quiet, surreptitious incursions.

A year later, I was in drama school. He was my friend. I was sitting in a group of black and white and Indian and people of colour university students at Wits in Johannesburg, saying 'up yours' to racial segregation. Bongani, whom I liked and trusted, arrived on the grass where we were resting in the shade, having lunch outside the drama department. He grabbed both my breasts in his hands, squeezing them. Then he sat down next to me.

I was in shock and crossed my hands over my chest. 'What the actual fuck?'

He smiled. 'What?'

'You can't just do that, Bongani,' I said. 'Jeez!'

'Why not?'

'What?'

'I'm just saying hi.'

'Bullshit.'

'I'm being friendly.'

I got up off the grass feeling awkward. The others looked at me. They smirked. I knew what they were thinking – she's so uptight. So uncool. I was. I didn't smoke or drink or smoke weed or do LSD or cocaine. I didn't sleep with all my girlfriends and boyfriends and think that having your breasts grabbed was oh-so-everyday. I felt sick. I walked away. Words lodged in my throat and never found a way out.

Back in the drama department building, I wanted to throw up. From that moment on, I gave him a wide berth.

South Africa has one of the highest rates of rape in the world, as I've said.

In 2011, a cross-sectional household study in South Africa done with a two-stage random sample of more than 1700 men aged between eighteen and forty-nine suggested that 27.6 per cent of them had raped a woman – either an intimate partner, stranger or acquaintance. 4.7 per cent of them had raped someone in the past twelve months. They'd all raped on multiple occasions.

Multiple occasions.

According to this study, men have motivations for rape that stem from a sense of sexual entitlement (Jewkes, 2011). And that runs north to south on our continent.

Bongani believed he was entitled to my breasts.

I ran away from Africa because statistically it was merely a matter of time before something random and far worse than having my breasts grabbed would transpire. I did not plan to stick around long enough for that.

*

As the Big Bad Patriarch found his way into your life in the form of harassment, but also in the form of mothers and aunties and grandmothers, so, too, did he come into my life in invisible ways.

*

In South Africa, the Panga Man was an indelible stain on every beautiful day when I was growing up. I was terrified of him. He was doubtless a warrior, skilled in the art of using a spear; he carried his panga (an axe) with him everywhere and he was responsible for murdering those who slept alone, or with others. All he needed was his panga. He beheaded the unwitting and kept their heads in a freezer in Zululand and made page four of the *Sunday Times* right at the bottom. He slit throats of sleeping innocents and robbed houses. His footprints were everywhere, but no matter how many times he was arrested, he spawned himself over and over again and committed crimes every minute. He hid in the bushes. He slipped into your house at night between the cracks, between the hinges of the door, and the doorframe. He slept in your bed and waited for you there. No broken-glass-topped high walls or alarm systems could keep him out. Days and nights were laced with the fear of this axe-wielding murderer since the moment I could first read the newspapers and found him between its pages.

Herschl was a nice Jewish boy. He grew up in a nice neighbourhood and he learned the violin and went to school. He was shy and wore glasses and came top of his class every time. A friend of my parents, he and his brothers were the nerds of the Jewish neighbourhood. Herschl grew up and married. He became a doctor, a respected local GP.

I met him one afternoon when I was at university. He was rehearsing with the Johannesburg Symphony Orchestra and he was in his thirties. The orchestra used the Great Hall for their rehearsals during the week.

I was just out of a lecture.

I walked through the hall and there he was, packing up his violin.

'Hi, Shelley.'

'Hi, Herschl. How are you?'

'Long time no see! You've grown up.'

'Yeah. What's happening?'

'Not much. Got divorced. Pretty messy. I'm a bit cut up about it.'

'I'm so sorry to hear that.'

'I'm not taking it very well,' he said, in soft, shy tones, pushing his glasses up higher on his nose.

'I'm sorry,' I said again, not wanting to be trapped talking to nerdy Herschl about his marital woes.

He left the orchestra and the next day and the day after, he went to work.

His ex-wife was a nurse. She worked in the general hospital, long night shifts, caring for the sick, the dying.

A short time after I saw Herschl, he woke up one morning and drove to the hospital where his ex-wife worked. He carried with him an axe. In the car park, he found his ex-wife's car, and smashed the windscreen, then the body of her car. And then he walked into the hospital, calm and cool. He knew where she was and he made his way down the corridors, and surprised her in a ward, where she stood, clipboard in hand.

And there, he hacked her to death. He did not hear her screams, her cries for mercy. And why no one could stop him, I will never know.

This Panga Man.

He was arrested and tried and convicted of murder and put in jail. He spent seven years there, a perfectly well-behaved prisoner. He managed the library.

When a family member visited him there, Herschl said that he had spoken to his therapist, who assured him that he did feel remorse for his deed.

As if he was a character in his own story. As if he had not soaked his hands in the blood of his once-beloved wife.

He was a model of good behaviour for seven years.

When he got out of jail, the Jewish Panga Man went back to practising medicine. Writing out prescriptions for antibiotics and listening to the lungs of young women and men. And playing the violin.

*

So why would it be surprising that Reza's fifteen-year-old son, whom she must have once loved more than life itself, took on the guise of the Big Bad Patriarch. A potential Panga Man.

Imagine.

Your own child.

Someone you would give your life for.

And this child becomes a monster and beats you orange and purple.

Many afternoons we had tea together. Or rice for dinner, Reza and Farhaz and Paul and Tim and I.

Farhaz was a polyglot. He read all the classics I gave him.

One day Reza said to me, 'Shelley, I have to tell you something. But this cannot go any further, and I tell you this, because I trust you. And in a way, I put my life in your hands. But I want you to know.'

What could I say but 'of course'.

And Reza said, 'I'm going back on holiday to Iran over the break. I have a sister in Sydney. I need to get from Iran to my sister in Sydney. But there are things that I need to do that are very hard. And I'm going to tell you this and say goodbye. When I go back to Iran, I'm going to leave my oldest there with his father, and a friend will help me get back to the airport. And please God, I will take Farhaz with me. And we will get on a plane. And we will fly to Australia. And I will never see those two – my husband and oldest son, again.'

I felt panic. And I swore secrecy.

It happened. The break came. Reza packed her things as if for a holiday. Her flat was cleaned, all her things still in it – all the boys' clothes and school books and belongings, the food in the fridge.

Reza stepped away from Qatar for a moment, a quick break – and then she was gone.

She did go back to Iran on holiday. When the new term started, she was not there. No Reza. No Farhaz. No more afternoons of tea or evenings of burnt rice and stories.

Some weeks later, I had news from her via a friend. Reza had gone back to Iran as planned; she had pretended to be back for a two-week holiday. And then one night she had fled under cover of darkness with Farhaz. They managed to get to the airport, where they boarded a plane. She made it to Sydney.

That's all I ever knew. That she made it to Sydney. I hope that she escaped the cruel hands of the Big Bad Patriarch. I imagine her living on this continent, free, in the sunshine. I imagine she and Farhaz took new names. I've searched for her on and off for years without luck. Maybe our paths have already crossed, in an airport, on a sidewalk in Sydney. Maybe the universe chuckled to itself at its own joke – look at these two, thrown back across one another's paths, after so many years and continents, and they don't even recognise each other.

Which is why I marvel at how the gossamer threads that tie you and me to one another pulled us back together in Oregon and London and Sydney and the Sunshine Coast over more than twenty years.

*

When Reza and Farhaz left Doha, my only close-to-the-heart people were you and Paul and Tim.

Paul was hired to play in a band in Doha and became the only lead guitarist in the whole country.

I stayed at home with the baby.

Paul began to make more money playing in the band than he made as a professor at the university. He told me about the extravagant parties at expat homes and embassies frequented by Qatari royalty. About the alcohol that flowed for everyone despite the ban on alcohol unless you were an expat with a permit. About the acres of food and the swimming pools and mansions the likes of which he'd never seen. Also, about a grand section of society made up of the rich, the politically connected, and the brothers-in-oil teams who operated above and beyond the law – a zone where bribes and *wasta* got people places.

Sometimes he came home after two in the morning.

'They threw a thousand dollars at each of us and asked us to play another hour.'

I didn't care about the money.

I didn't know what to do with a life lived in a light green apartment looking out over the Gulf and the dust.

I stood at the window looking out at Al Rayan Road which roared past our block of flats. I rocked Tim to sleep on my shoulder. I watched men in white and women in black, their tent-shapes silhouetted against the blue waters of the Arabian Gulf in winter. The shallow salty sea stretched out to Palm Tree Island, a place for tourists – you could take a boat there if you wanted – but it was not much of a place for women. Nowhere was. And I thought, *this is my life.*

Before social isolation was a global experience, women living in the Middle East were experts at it. And I began to learn the art of Being Alone Inside.

# 21.

# SHAIMAA

I envy you
The poise
 Your steps that know their way
 Your rare startles and surprises
 The ease of your beauty
 The lack of need to impress
 Your know-how
 The respect you command
 Merely by existing
 Your calm smile
 I look at you and I envy you
 What mistakes have you made?
 Have they made you doubt yourself?
 Oh, I've made a few!
 And I envy you
 Your wide-eyedness
 Your innocence despite your years
 The wisdom you long for
 It's already in you
 Your grace as you get up

And try again
The endless possibilities
The surprises in store
The relentless need to move forward
Your youth, your energy, your vigour
The beauty you can't see
The confidence you think you lack
The near future
Where you scorn perfection
The journey to know yourself
I look at you and I envy you

# 22.

# SHELLEY

At night the sky over Doha turned deep purple. Above the parapets of the *Al Jazzi* (*Al Snazzy*) compound and the nearby mosque, the upside-down Arabian moon hung in the sky like an ironic smile – sideways.

The colours I saw from the windows of Dafna apartments – I would like to describe them. But what is the colour of dust? Before the purple, and the upside-down moon, the sky at sunset is the colour of burnt rice, not at the middle, where it's darkest, but towards the edges, where the rice turns gold-brown up the side of the pot.

No rain. No birds. Sometimes in the evenings, the sound of building and construction starting up as the heat subsided somewhat, as if the whole desert was a quarry. Between Dafna and the Corniche was an open space of rubble. I watched men in that pile of rocks and dust, perhaps from Pakistan or India, out there in their clothes turned orange with dust, hewing rocks with mallets that they swung over their shoulders. They did this year-round – in the summer, even, when the temperatures reached fifty-seven degrees sometimes. The call to prayer. Traffic. The taste of dust.

Back then, I wanted to try to put into words that world of dust and rocks and fifty-seven degrees Celsius. But I was afraid then, as I am now, that anything I wrote might be misconstrued as affirming the Grand Western Narrative of the superiority of Western ways of being and knowing over Middle Eastern, or African, or any other way of being and knowing.

But writing between your words dissolves me. The places I fear to reach into happen between the words. Runaways look for safety, not exposure. Born a certain race, onto a certain continent, in a certain time – we are interlined by history and geography. Jews are separated from Muslims, Christians from Jews and Muslims, black people from white, men from women – these lines, they would sever you from me if they had their way.

I am saved by your story – by being tangled in it. Because we love things, and people and places together, through time, across continents, there is no danger of a single story, a single reality. You help me to feel whole. To see my story as valid, a thread in an intricately woven terrain of our intersecting lives.

Because the single uniting human factor is that we are primed for freedom.

And I will push back against anything that keeps me or you bound or gagged – I will resist any threat to squash us small. I wish to go back in time and stand against anything that wishes to diminish you or make you quiet.

# 23.

# SHAIMAA

The story of you in that place at that time is safe with me. I've always felt that you were trying to understand. You were a young mother, fighting her own battles with a new baby – the physical, mental and emotional struggles – while trying to function as a professional. All in a place that seemed so strange to you. You were trying to understand why men felt it was their right to follow you home and harass you or push your car off the road, or make you feel like you were confined to your Dafna flat. Of segregated men's and women's campuses.

I was a young woman – a teenager – ready to be in the world, live and experience new things. I landed in a place where women mainly stayed indoors, to not brave the streets. A place that afforded my family a better lifestyle and financial resources. But took away our sense of settlement and security. 'Our bags are just on that cupboard,' my mum would joke. 'When they tell us to go, we'll go.' To her it was something she expected and was willing to deal with. To me it was a threat: *You see what you have now? We can take it away anytime. We can send you back home.* That was always my irk with Doha. That I could never get comfortable even in a place that offered comfort. That I could never really feel secure. It was the catch-22 of all time. Not feeling secure at home because of lack of opportunity and financial prospects and not feeling secure in the Gulf because of the transient nature of the place experienced by those who moved and worked there.

Yours and mine are stories of two women who landed in a place that was foreign to them to varying degrees. To me this is about both of us understanding an experience which we had to survive, adapt to and eventually walk away from. It's about understanding these surroundings and understanding what we were going through in them. I am grateful. My Doha experience, as foreign and confined as it was, it has given me so much and has, in many ways, propelled me forward. Doha was my first escape. Even though it wasn't a conscious decision I made, I was following my family.

But it was the first time that I realised that my relationship with my homeland was best lived from a distance. That I would rather miss home than be stifled by it.

Doha afforded me the opportunity to know and befriend those who were different from me. To love the rest of the Middle East through my friendships. It taught me that women can work with and around any restrictions and still find laughter and life even behind closed doors and high gates. It was a different kind of intimacy, one that I wasn't used to. Doha also meant that I met you and your beautiful small family.

I'm so grateful to you and for you.

You are the loving midwife to those words of mine. Those words ... The most stubborn of babies!

I feel that my writing is a perpetual overdue pregnancy! Painful and irritating to keep in. And excruciating to get out. I do realise I've just used a baby metaphor. The irony is not lost on me – the very person who sent you a poem with 'I don't dream of my child's face – I dare to tell her we won't meet'.

Mind you, words are the only things I'm willing to birth.

I understand that I know nothing about bringing a child into this world or the pain that it entails. I do know, however, about the pain of trying to get pregnant. Trying and failing at the thing that was expected of me and which I was told was the most natural thing to want. Except deep down I knew, I just *knew* I didn't want it. And yet it defined at least the first seven years of my marriage.

Then the million questions from family and friends. The unsolicited advice from women I'd only just met about the best time in the month to have sex. What to eat. Lose weight. Gain weight. The best gynaecologists Egypt had to offer. That thing that a second cousin of someone's mother tried after five years and got pregnant. That story of a friend of a friend who finally had a baby ten years into her marriage and now she's very happy and it was all okay. The *don't worry it will happen for you believe me you just need to keep trying and praying. You need to pray more.*

Everybody was an expert. It was the extended stake that everyone had in my body which clearly wasn't doing what it was there to do.

Then IVF. I was considered obese for an NHS-funded treatment so I had to lose weight to be considered. I remember going to the gynaecologist's office and him weighing me, registering the number and saying, 'That's not the right number. Your BMI still too high. That's not good, Shaimaa. You need to lose more weight to be considered. Let's keep trying. That's if you want to go on that list.'

I'd always been body-shamed for gaining weight and ruining my figure. For giving up on thinness and allowing my bulges to bulge. How I let myself down by losing my membership in the Thin People's Club which I entered for only one summer before eating myself into the Obesity Zone. I'd grown used to, if not less hurt by, those comments about how everything was going to be better once I lost weight. Not in a million years did I think that included being a mother too.

I wasn't only failing at having a child, I was now failing at being thin enough to be considered safe to try for a child. I finally lost enough weight – a mix of starving myself, living on those shake and soup powder programs and purging every now and then.

'Great news,' the doctor said. 'The weight is right and the BMI numbers are good. We can now start the IVF process,' he announced to me, looking at me quizzically when he saw that I wasn't excited by the news.

I was tired of it all by then and I hadn't even started. It dawned on me to ask the doctor whether he wanted to know how I lost the weight and whether he thought the way I lost it was healthier than the way I'd gained it. I wanted to know why I was only considered 'healthy' when I was thin regardless of how I became thin. Why was my 'health' less acceptable only when I was fat – even though the road to both had nothing to do with well-being. But we'd come this far.

The process started with a meeting at the nurse's office. A whole demonstration for me and my husband (no idea why) of what we (there was no we in this) needed to do, which hormones needed to be injected when, where and how. 'Find a good bit of fat in your tummy or bottom,' she said.

'That won't be a problem,' I thought. 'There's plenty of that hanging about.'

The injections had to be accurately timed. One in the morning, one at night as far as I remember. I had to take the whole kit to work with me when I was on early shifts, go into the bathroom at work, find a good bit of fat in my tummy that hadn't already been pricked and poked, and inject myself.

Even trickier was travelling on work assignments with all that good stuff! Explaining the syringes and ampules to border officers at the departures security gates was a real treat with the rest of the crew watching. I want to think that none of them paid attention and thankfully no one asked. One of the more surreal moments was being in Saudi Arabia on a shoot – one of my earlier field production trips – calculating the time difference between Jeddah and London to check when to inject myself with those hormones which had been wreaking havoc on my insides physically and mentally, then going out to work with the reporter and cameraman in one of the most difficult countries to report from!

I was surprised at how well I worked those syringes. I got good at the whole injections thing. I wouldn't have thought I'd be able to do it, but I did. For two glorious IVF rounds. Pumping myself with hormones, overwhelming every bit of my being, all in pursuit of motherhood. This thing I was supposed to be seeking, that was supposed to feel natural. This was the second time I went through the 'extraction' phase (these are not technical terms obviously). I went under full anaesthetic so they could take the 'good eggs' out to fertilise them with what the hubby has offered in a plastic cup earlier.

'Well done, Shaimaa,' the doctor said as I came to, still groggy. 'Nine good ones.'

Then came the other procedure I had to go through: 'insertion'. No anaesthetic this time. The fertilised eggs now went back in with the hope they'd turn into an embryo. Which would hopefully decide to stay and become a baby.

I don't remember much except that I was supposed to drink water to fill my bladder as that made it easier for the procedure. I was sitting there waiting for my turn, desperate to go to the bathroom. Dreading the rest of it. I'd done it before. I knew it would involve the doctor pulling my legs apart and pushing that cold speculum inside me and opening wide to insert my potential baby. That thing that was meant to bring me joy.

I broke down in the waiting room. I cried because I felt desperate and pathetic. Then I felt pathetic because I cried. I cried because here I was, a woman in my mid-thirties dying to pee, my bladder and my heart about to burst. I didn't know how and why I got there – to this feeling, to that waiting room. I cried because I felt beaten by this thing that everyone else wanted for me.

I continued to cry as I lay down with my legs open. The doctor said she understood that this was all 'uncomfortable' as she shoved the speculum inside me. For an invasive and rather cruel device, the speculum is quite funny-looking. It looks like a duck. An evil, cold metal duck that gets into your vagina and opens its mouth wide so the doctors can do what they need to do.

'Now you wait,' was the simple instruction. 'If you bleed it's failed. If you don't – take a pregnancy test. Then come and see the doctor.' That was the bottom line told to us in a more understated technical fashion.

How was this natural? I kept thinking. How was I supposed to feel right now, about what was inside me. That thing was either going to be a blotch of blood in a pad or a potential person to be born.

I know I felt exhausted, angry and confused – but none of it felt natural.

And then came the blotch of blood. That warm thick red alert slipping from inside me, telling me in no uncertain terms that I had failed. That whatever was inside me wasn't going to stick around. And there I was left shedding embryo remains, uterus lining and lots and lots of tears.

It wasn't a sense of loss. I wasn't grieving anything. It was a bruise. A failure. I had that thing on my Female To-Do List, and instead of a green check, I got a big red 'F' next to it. Twice. I had failed at what was expected of me. I had failed at this thing I wasn't sure I wanted.

'It's okay,' my husband said. 'We'll try again. Some couples go through ten of these before they get pregnant.'

'You mean I. I will try again,' I said.

There's no *we* when I shoot myself up every day with hormones that turn me inside out. There's no *we* when I get eggs taken out of me and inserted back into me. And I'm not doing it again.

'No,' I found myself saying to him. 'I'm not doing it again. I'm not trying again. I'm done. I don't want children.'

I could see he was hurt. He calmly said we shouldn't make any decisions when this was so fresh and painful. But I realised I had made that decision long before I said it. I had made that decision when I knew that this wasn't something I wanted or longed for. Everything about motherhood filled me with dread and anxiety. It was not something I was looking for or forward to. It was something I had to do and failing at it had actually freed me to say out loud that I didn't want it. At least to myself and my husband.

All these years later I still wouldn't dare say that to my mother or to the rest of my or Ahmed's family. I hide behind the sob story. I use my failure as cover for one of the most liberating things I've found out about myself, but that is still unacceptable for a woman to say openly.

I'm not anti-children. I would die for my nephews and niece. I love them with all my heart. I respect any woman's choice to have children as long as she knows it's a choice and a difficult one. What I am against are the lies. The expectations. The lies that motherhood is a natural state of being and the expectation that it's an inherent yearning and that it happens for everyone. It's not and it doesn't.

The lies about the neatness. That mums don't suffer. That those in pursuit of being mums don't suffer. That every woman has to be a mother. That a woman can give birth and bounce off to a gym the next day. The narrative about childbirth (which I have no right to talk about I know) that lacks truth about sleep deprivation, bleeding, infections, loss of self and rage. I've seen it happen to my sister. She tried to explain this to me so many times. I never really understood. The contrast confused me. The suffering from a wrecked body after labour, coupled with the pleasure of holding her child. Then, as they grew older, the draining morning runs, the daily arguments about homework and chores, coupled with humour and laughter. The messiness of the house and the liveliness of a home. The life the children have brought to her and drained out of her all at once.

# 24.

# SHELLEY

Your experience undoes me.
Also, I'm exhilarated. That you found your voice.
The word least heard when women say it.
No.

No, to the making of you into a vessel for other's wishes, desires, expectations. No, to you losing yourself to the lies. You didn't. You haven't.

I love that.

*

I want to tell you about losing myself. About losing love in the Arabian desert. How it happened slowly – eating away from the inside.

In that desert the hours stretched out, elongated by the heat. Sometimes I would look at my watch in horror that only five minutes had gone by, when it felt like I'd been breastfeeding for years.

Afterbirth – it happens for years, decades, maybe a lifetime.

The shockwaves go out far, waves into the universe, rippling through time.

Afterbirth is separate to the child – and the intense love. I loved my baby more than my life.

But giving life to another human results inevitably of some destruction of the host.

It's the Way Things Are in Nature.

Afterbirth.

The midwife who stitched me up had never had a baby.

'I hate suturing,' she said, sticking a thick needle into my burning broken perineum. I said stop. She didn't. The pain was blinding. 'I can feel everything,' I said. 'You should still be numb,' she said. I'm NOT NUMB! I was never numb!

She insisted I should still be numb. As if that would make it so.

And she wasn't a good seamstress. This one who hated suturing.

Eventually I slammed my legs together. After the last stitch.

It's as though you open your mouth to yawn and when you close it again your jaw is permanently dislocated. Your bottom lip protrudes to the side. This is your new face.

The bad seamstress did not line up the two sides of my perineum. There was an extra flap of skin with nowhere to go. It sucked energy, this thing.

What was it, originally?

In Qatar, who was there to talk to about the extra flap of skin?

I thought it wasn't as bad as my young student who had to fly to London to get 'fixed' after she was left in a 'mess' by her doctors in Qatar.

The pain and discomfort turned the days colourless.

My gentle husband's body looked different.

As did mine.

'It's scary,' he said, looking at me.

'Not as scary as yours,' I said, looking at him. I was a deflated balloon. He was an invader capable of causing pain and destruction.

Flaps of skin. Destroyed muscles.

Orgasms became a flutter – a nothingness. Eros fled.

Breasts were working pumps – nourishing new life. The compulsion to be there for the existence of the child I loved so much was beyond my own need for survival.

In the long, long hours breastfeeding, my soul fled.

I ran away. In my dreams, my nightmares.

I said to Paul, 'Don't touch me. I don't know who I even am.'

He told me it was traumatic contemplating that eroticism and sexuality were just an evolutionary trick to get us to do this thing.

He told me about a girl he'd met since he recently joined the theatre group the Doha Players; they were doing *Little Shop of Horrors*, and this girl, or maybe woman, she was English, and a really good singer. The way he talked – he was inspired. Animated. I asked him about her. In five minutes I became obsessed. How old is she? What does she look like? There was too much energy around her and I feared he liked her. She's just a singer, he said. She's not important in my life.

This is how love gets lost.

We sat there on the couch, looking at the desert.

'I don't know if I love you anymore,' he said.

'Me neither.'

I choked on heartbreak. He was sorry, he said.

'You could have told me this before my body was destroyed. Before we did this.'

'I'm sorry. But whatever we feel, we have no choice but to make this work. We have a baby to look after,' he said.

*

And then he went out again, several nights a week, to play in the musical, to play in the band, to hang out with the millionaires and I feared, to flirt with the spoiled daughters of oil magnates.

No therapists. No counsellors.

Maybe in the *Al Jazzi* compound. Or the Gulf Helicopter Compound where the bass guitarist from Paul's band lived.

But not in Dafna where I was given a taste of what life was like for my desert sisters, floating in a void, in a place where women's voices vanished in the dust and men got on with their lives, oblivious to the sea of blood and tears on which they stood so casually day in, day out.

Anger grew.

Paul's life grew more and more different from mine.

Everyone loved him. He could go anywhere he wanted at any time. I couldn't and I didn't.

I lost myself.

I taught my classes and I rushed home to feed my baby.

He came home late from playing in the band, in musicals, dripping in good spirits and community and camaraderie.

The anger of afterbirth grew fat in the desert.

Who had we become?

I raged inwardly at the conspiracy of silence. I relived childbirth in my dreams over and over. I wanted to rip the magazines about mothers and motherhood and babies, the pink and blue ribbons, to shreds. The quasi-erotic breastfeeding pictures. Their presence silencing the stories of the torn and wrongly sewn-up vulvas, the cracked and bleeding nipples, the infected breasts, the vomiting during labour, the near-death pain of giving birth, the way a body once primed for pleasure turns itself inside out and becomes in the process of mothering, the lodging and the food of the next generation.

You are so brave. I admire you. Your looking away from the face of a not-born child. Your freedom is to choose to not lay yourself waste. Your body is your sanctuary. Yours. And you had to fight hard to have it.

I want our other stories out. The understories. The ones that don't make the front covers of *Mother and Baby* magazines, or even the last page; the ones that don't fill our heads with orgasmic descriptions of labour and birth in blue pools with soft music playing where husbands kiss the sweaty brows of gorgeously labouring women and amidst after birth and tears and more sweet music, babies latch on to breasts and gently draw sustenance from their mothers; let out the stories that the girls in the labour ward of the local hospital will never tell, and the others like mine that people will resist because they dissect the myths of our time and ruin the Grand Narrative that Motherhood is the Most Natural Thing in the World and It Makes You Fulfilled. *Motherhood is NOT the Most Natural Thing in the World.* Also, where are the medals – the honours, the goddamn trumpets – for the women, the ones who are going to war every day and putting their bodies and lives on the line, so that sometimes, others might live?

One night, Paul and I awoke with the sound of a loud explosion.

We ran out, bleary-eyed onto the balcony.

In the strange night, illuminated by the orange streetlights along Al Rayan Road, the new building between us and the Corniche looked to be awkwardly off-centre.

Another ear-drum-shattering sound.

The smell of concrete.

I inhaled dust. As if in slow motion, the building collapsed in on itself. A crane, caught in the fall, tipped over. A plume of orange spiralled into the night.

My heart raced. 'That building,' I said. 'That whole building! It just fell down. The workers ...'

'Let's go inside,' Paul said.

'No, I want to see it,' I said. I knew I was looking at someone's death that night. The clouds grew bigger. More slabs of concrete collapsed.

'Come on,' he said, and drew me back inside.

We sat in the lounge in the hours between midnight and sunrise. 'People were in there working,' I said. Paul made me camomile tea.

'I know,' he said.

'I want to leave,' I said.

'I know,' he said.

'You're becoming like them,' I said.

'Like who?'

'Like all the other men here. The ones who think it's okay that their wives stay at home in these boxes.'

'I don't think it's okay. I'm not like those men. I don't want you to feel like this. But it's the only job I've found.'

'I know. But help me.'

He hugged me and held me. I cried. For the love that hung there, an extra flap of skin ... no one remembered quite where it came from, and what to do with it, now that it was just hanging in no-man's-land.

And I cried for the mothers. For the children. For those who weren't mothers. For the poor slave-workers from Pakistan doing the building at night to avoid the heat of the day, until it fell on them because it was poorly constructed and building codes were lax or easily pushed aside – and they died there, those men, beneath the rubble.

'I need you to love me again,' I said.

'I do love you,' he said.

'But you said you didn't.'

'You also said you didn't. I didn't mean it. It wasn't true.'

'It felt true,' I said.

'Things changed,' he said. 'It was hard to see you go through that. I didn't know how to deal with it.'

'I feel ruined and you're in a distant galaxy moving away at the speed of light. I was always terrified of being a cliché. And now we are.'

'We can change things,' he said.

*

I had one escape: the Sheraton Beach Club.

A singularity.

That pyramid-shaped hotel on the blue waters of the Arabian Gulf, with its white sand beaches, mimicked the reality of tropical islands where women walked freely clad in bikinis and did not have to pay an astronomical fee just to sit on soft grass grown with great effort and watered at great cost. I began to dream of an escape to a place where Tim could lie down on the ground and see real trees, watch birds flying free, ducking and weaving through branches, spreading their wings to catch thermals, singing at the top of their lungs.

That lone bird in its cage at the Sheraton, a rainbow lorikeet, was a prisoner and I hated looking at it. Yet it was a creature so startling that Tim's first word as we walked past the cage one day and he reached out his hand, was 'bir'.

I felt like my life was being lived out on a limited movie set in a show at the end of the world.

*

How to find love lost in the desert:

1. Make an oasis. You will have to use sewage and grey water to make things grow; you will have to fertilise the flowers with your own waste; there will be nothing for nothing.

2. Take care of the oasis. There will be no rain for three years and if you forget to water it and fertilise it, everything will shrivel and dry up and starting it again will be much harder the second time around.

3. Spend time in the oasis. There's no point going to all that effort if you're not going to sometimes just sit there and enjoy the colours and the spurts of beauty that will invariably appear.

The Sheraton membership cost the equivalent of a full month's salary.

# 25.

# SHAIMAA

God, the silence. This damn silence. To lose yourself in every way all at once: woman, wife, lover at the altar of Motherhood. To have that happen and watch the person you love draw further and further away, embraced by an outside world that rejects and is hostile to everything about you. To watch him flourish while you fade in a strange land. It was like the place and circumstances were competing on who was going to suck the life out of you faster. Were the endless, empty, dust-filled Doha days and nights going to do it? Or was it your decimated body that you were desperate to keep together to feed your child going to get there first? It feels like both your soul and vagina were slashed open and weren't stitched up right ... leaving extra flappy bits with nowhere to go.

And that building collapsing! Gosh could there be a more poignant metaphor to how you were feeling inside?

Was that the night you decided to leave? I'm in awe of how you took your life back. How you reclaimed your love, your pain, your right to your anger and to more from life. I'm astounded at how you managed to separate and protect your love for your child from all of this. Many childhood traumas start from traumatised mums. And here you were on the verge of collapsing yet you kept yourself and that love together.

I've been lucky enough to visit your Oasis. That lovely manicured, overpriced artificial piece of nature and freedom that made me breathe differently when I was in it. I can see how it was important to keep you sane. You needed a sanctuary even if you had to pay a month's salary to sit on some grass.

And I know that for you to do that you had to run away …

# 26.

# SHELLEY

Everything around me crumbled. Or perhaps it was I that was crumbling.

I wrote, while in Qatar, mostly children's and young adult novels set in Africa. The books were accepted and published quickly. When my copies arrived in the mail, they had been censored. Sometimes the illustrations in the children's books had been blacked out with a big black marker. Girl characters wearing sleeveless tops were scribbled over. My new hot-off-the-press author's copies arrived looking like they were ten years old and like a three-year-old had had a go with a stolen marker.

I noticed that as the months went by, more and more of my women students were covered. When I first started teaching, only two out of the hundred and ten women were completely covered – as in, I couldn't see their eyes, which were behind a net. After that first year and a half, there were maybe ten. Eventually almost everyone on the women's side wore some kind of hijab. You were one of the few without one.

In fifty-seven degrees Celsius, I wore a long-sleeved black jacket and long black trousers and black shoes to work. I wore my hair in a tight hair-crab and wore dark sunglasses that were too big for me and covered a third of my face.

I was walking from class to my car when Dr Johara called to me.

'Mrs Shelley!' she said.

I stopped. 'Yes?'

'I want to tell you something.'

'Sure.'

She looked me up and down. 'Your trousers, Mrs Shelley.'

'Pardon?'

'Your trousers. Our girls look at you, and it offends them. That you are wearing trousers. It's not a good example for them. Please, Mrs Shelley. Your trousers.'

Her eyes pleaded with me. I shifted my bag to my other shoulder and blinked away the sweat that slid down my face, my neck.

'Dr Johara, I am not being disrespectful. I am covered from head to toe. I wear my trousers because they are comfortable, and because they are what I would easily wear to work in the West. If you hire someone from another place, they bring not just their language, but also a little bit of their culture. This is a little bit of my culture. I would respectfully wear these trousers to work in America, or England, or South Africa. But I will ask every class I teach if they're offended, and if any single girl is offended by my trousers, I will stop wearing them.'

She went quiet. She nodded sadly. She had failed to impress upon me something that was deeply disturbing her. I just could not acquiesce.

In that week, true to my word, I asked all five classes of women if wearing trousers offended them. The students laughed. No, they said. I feel sure they would have told me.

'We love that you wear trousers,' Hend said. 'It's who you are.'

And so, I continued to wear them, and Dr Johara looked at me on a daily basis with resignation and disappointment.

My covered women students. When my female students spoke I never saw their mouths move – but I knew their voices. And I loved them, though many I never saw.

Women the world over are more likely to be interrupted, silenced, misunderstood and misheard than men.

My classes were noisier and chattier than most.

And I let it happen. Here was one place where the sounds of their voices would not be silenced. Their musical tones would ring out maybe across the desert, maybe into far distant hills, maybe eventually loosing water from hidden places beneath the rocks, causing a flood. I could only imagine.

Meanwhile, I was restless.

I heard from a colleague – yet another rumour – that in Saudi the previous Friday, a young mother was beheaded for starting a feminist movement. I cannot find any reference to this today, so it's hard to know whether this was true, but in 2018 NBC News reported that, 'In a first, Saudi prosecutors are seeking to behead a female activist for participating in anti-government protests, according to rights campaigners.'* It's possible that there was truth in the terrible rumour back then.

I went to class on the women's side the next day. I had never said anything like this.

'Can you ladies tell me: do honour killings still happen here, in your society, in your lives?'

'Yes,' they said. 'Yes, they do, Mrs Shelley.'

My anger grew larger than my fear. 'Young women here are killed by their fathers and husbands and brothers if they're suspected, even just suspected of having anything to do with another man?'

---

* https://www.nbcnews.com/news/world/saudi-arabia-seeks-unprecedented-death-penalty-woman-activist-n902771

'Yes Mrs Shelley,' someone said at the back. 'Of course.' As if I were stupid.

'But … do you think that's right? Do you?' I'm sure I sounded too loud, too emotional, bordering on the unprofessional.

'It's not right, but it is our way,' Huda, at the back, said.

I must have looked stunned.

'Mrs Shelley,' Huda said. 'No disrespect intended. We know you are older than we are, and you probably know a lot more than we do in many ways – but sometimes we think you are much younger than us, like a child because of the amount that you do not understand.'

*

In 2019, a young woman in Melbourne met a young man in a bar and they went for a late-night stroll in Royal Park. The next day twenty-five-year-old Courtney Herron was found brutally bashed to death. Henry Hammond was arrested for her murder, but due to mental illness, schizophrenia, and being psychotic at the time, he was found not guilty and was committed to a psychiatric hospital for twenty-five years. He beat Courtney to death with a tree branch because he believed she had wronged his family in a past life. A year before that, Eurydice Dixon was killed nearby in Princes Park by a stranger. Natalina Angok was killed by her boyfriend Christopher Bell, also a schizophrenic. A few months before that, Aiia Maasarwe, who was just 21, was attacked and murdered near La Trobe University – at the hands of a strange man. This is just Melbourne, a safe, liveable city in a safe, liveable country. It's hard for me to comprehend that in Australia, every week, let's put it this way, at least one man murders a woman, often a former spouse or girlfriend. After Courtney's death, assistant Commissioner Luke Cornelius told reporters that 'violence against women is absolutely about men's behaviour'.

Well, yes.

*

I start to think that the Middle East is the perfect scapegoat for the West when it comes to the silencing and destruction of women. If we stand on the West side and point our fingers at the women of the Arabian Gulf, for example, and say, *look, their mouths are covered, their faces are covered, they can look out, but that's it* – if we say that, then we can look away from the dead women beneath the ground in Australia.

In the desert, history and culture amplifies these crimes and makes us shiver. In the Middle East, the cruelties experienced by women are gigantic shadows projected onto the sand in harsh light – the abuse, the silencing, the subjugation, even killings that can be 'honourable' and beheadings of young mothers in front of crowds. The horrendous crimes perpetrated against women in the Middle East allow the West to go, *Look, look how bad it is over there. You're so lucky not to live there. You're so lucky to be free.* But the freedom is a veneer and it's relative. Women are still dying in the West at the hands of men – because they are women. They are talked over, the evolutionary fact of softer, weaker, penetrable bodies against a stronger, harder, less penetrable design ensures subjugation. Yet, it is generally the mark of an evolved society that it protects the physically more vulnerable and holds those physically stronger to account.

The West creates the Middle East in its own shadow.

I have been trying to outrun it.

Women the world over have been trying to outrun it. The #MeToo movement has carved out a space that maybe wasn't there before. Perhaps female voices have grown louder – perhaps there is more airtime devoted to women now than there was twenty years ago – they can call out the crimes that are being committed against them to some degree – but even in my close circles, friends of friends and people I know, there is a shocking amount of violent coercive behaviour towards women by men who are supposed to be 'enlightened'. I fear that female runaways will be searching for safety until the law in every part of the world stops being the long, hairy arm of the Big Bad Patriarch, and until boys are brought up to be gentle and compassionate.

We hedge our bets – women everywhere. I weighed up risk and benefit: in Qatar, I was safer, for example, than in South Africa. In South Africa I had a one in three chance of being raped, a one in four of being infected with HIV if I was raped, unless I was murdered. I had a high risk of being hijacked. Between 50 and 60 people a day are hijacked and often killed for their cars.

In Qatar, I was hounded home and ridden into the desert.

I didn't fear hijackings.

I wondered about kidnappings.

But I was a runaway. And I chose the Middle East over Africa, for survival. If that was a real choice.

According to the NSW Rape Crisis Centre, 35 per cent of ALL women in the world have experienced sexual violence at the hands of their intimate partners in most instances. The worst regions are the Middle East and South-East Asia (37.7 per cent of women have been affected), Africa (36.6 per cent), the Americas (29.8 per cent), and Australia, New Zealand, the US, Canada, members of the European Union, Israel, South Korea and Japan (23.2 per cent) – though according to *Our Watch*, 34.2 per cent of Australian women have experienced physical and/or sexual violence perpetrated by a man since age fifteen.

We know that stats on women's abuse are grossly under-reported – more so in countries like Qatar than in the developed world, but still, 25 per cent of Australian women have been abused, versus 5 per cent of men. Women are hospitalised daily here, in our safe and beautiful country which seems such a far cry from a place where a close relative might slit your throat for looking at a boy.

In Qatar, after finding out about the shadows under which my young women students lived, I did not know how to breathe the air in that room where those women had to exist with the ever-present threat of honour killings over their heads.

Shaimz, you've been close to them, these women students. Did they confide in you ever? Were you privy to the marbled and gilded lives lived by those who were wealthy and yet so restricted?

You've reported on at least one high-profile honour killing in Pakistan, for example, because the woman came home from the UK to visit, or so she thought. You've looked into the eyes of the husband and father who were accused of killing that woman, and you've written the stories. But I want to know where the heaviness of the story goes afterwards. I wonder how you carry it.

# 27.

# SHAIMAA

My sister and I had a conversation once in London that always stayed with me. She was visiting and we were on the train going to the city. I'd noticed a sign on the seats in front of us saying they were designated for disabled people, pregnant women or the elderly.

I pointed it out and said that this was why I loved living here. That there was always consideration for the less able and the vulnerable. That everyone was guaranteed a place on public transport and the right to get around in dignity and independence.

'True. This is great. But at what cost?' she asked.

'What do you mean?'

'I mean this is all nice. The West gets to be supportive of human rights and women's rights and disabled rights but what about the other humans, the other women and the other disabled people in the rest of the world. Do they care about their rights? Think about it,' she said. 'Think how hard it is for refugees or economic immigrants to come to this country! They gave me such a hard time just for a visit visa to come to this conference. You yourself wouldn't be here if it weren't for Ahmed's job.'

True. But I was confused. Why was making sure that the elderly and the less abled had a place on public transport bad? We don't see this where we come from. We see it here in Western countries. That was a good thing, right?

'You know what this is like?' she tried to explain. 'It's like those really expensive compounds back home in Egypt. My husband and I spent all our savings trying to secure a house in one of them. What are they selling?'

'Space. Safety. Green areas. Swimming pools.' I listed.

'Exclusivity,' she said.

She was right. The only way any of those things were valuable was because they were surrounded by high walls and secure gates.

The only way to maintain the dream world inside is to keep it closed to those outside. Life was good ONLY to those who could afford to live in the compound.

But by doing that, by gating the greenery, the safe walkways and the swimming pools, we inherently tell those who can't afford them they have no right to them.

\*

The West is the gated compound of the world. Only if you cross the high walls and the impenetrable borders do you get to enjoy the compound's amenities of freedom, safety and equality. And even that is not guaranteed for everyone equally.

Everyone here has rights because everyone is well … HERE.

But what about those who are not? What rights do they have? And if they didn't have those rights in their homelands, were they welcome to seek them here in this country, on this train with the designated seats?

If you weren't lucky enough to be born in a country that values human rights, freedom of expression and women's place in society, are you still entitled to them?

For whichever reason, I've ended up inhabiting both spaces. The one within the gates of the beautiful compound and the other outside.

When I'm in my home country in the East I'm reminded of everything I ran away from – the crushing pressure to assimilate, to lose my individuality in tradition and expectation.

And when I'm in the West, the place I ran to, I'm reminded of my otherness. My inability to belong despite fitting in.

I found this letter/list of questions to the West in one of my very old notebooks. I can claim that I've understood the complexity of some of the answers, but I can't claim I have all of them.

Dear West,
- Are you a real place or are you an illusion of a promise of safety, stability and freedom?
- Are you aware of the lives lost in the name of spreading your values?
- Are some lives really more equal than others?
- Can you claim that your wealth is yours and yours alone if it was built on the exploitation of people and resources in other countries that you've since left derelict with a legacy of tyranny and corruption?
- Can you claim to be a beacon of democracy when you're still struggling with racism and you've backed dictators in other countries who oppress their people and violate their rights only to then start wars to topple those dictators when they don't suit your geopolitical goals for total control of resources?
- How have you sold us this dream? How have you become the place we all want to escape to from the things you've condoned or helped create?
- How do I love you and feel so betrayed by you?

When you've lived long enough in the lovely gated compound, you then start to see chinks in its armour.

The pools aren't as blue, the gardens not as lush green as they are in the brochure.

To this day, in the UK and USA, men get paid more than women for doing the exact same jobs. Black and ethnic minorities still struggle to get to leading positions in big institutions and industries, they still suffer some form of racism every day. Many have been targeted by the police.

In the midst of a global pandemic, some women are stuck at home in the 'developed world' in fear of another episode of domestic violence.

In my new home, the one I ran to, it has taken a young footballer, Marcus Rashford of Manchester United, to fight child food poverty. Children are going hungry in the UK and the government was planning to take away their food vouchers.

In the United States, kids now go through mass-shooting drills. Other children are separated from their parents at the border and kept in cages.

\*

In my new work home, Australia, Indigenous people are the most incarcerated in the world by percentage of their population. If you're an Aboriginal teenage boy in the 'Lucky Country', you're more likely to go to jail than to go to university.

There's no doubt that the struggles of people, especially women, in my region and my country are real. Oppression is real, violence against women is real. But the West has its own very real issues too.

In 2020 in the USA a white police officer pinned a black man face-down on the ground in handcuffs and pressed his knee against his neck until the black man died crying out for his mother.

\*

Yes, I've found what I was looking for in the West or the developed world: freedom, equality, diversity, human rights. I can't deny that ever. But I've also realised how hollow these notions can be when put to the test sometimes.

If you'd told me that as part of my Australia Correspondent job, I'd be covering a women's march calling out sexual violence and misogyny outside Parliament House, I wouldn't have believed you.

And yet there I was speaking to women of all ages. All angry and fed up, all telling me their different stories of sexual harassment on the streets, in bars, at their workplaces.

One of the speakers at the rally told me that she came as a refugee from Sierra Leone where she was raped during the civil war.

'I came here to feel safe. It's shocking that this is happening here. I can't believe I have to talk to Australian women about this still!' she told me.

A little girl was holding a big placard and it made me shudder. 'I'm eleven and I've had enough of harassment.' Eleven. The same age I went through the exact same thing for the first time.

It was happening everywhere. At the same time women were taking to the streets in London where a young woman named Sarah Everard was killed as she walked home one night.

Women in the developed world were crying out, wanting to reclaim the streets, demanding safety – a cry that has been muffled and repressed for decades in the region I came from. How was this happening here? Wasn't this the 'Safe Place'? Hasn't the West long lectured people of my region, chastising us about how barbarically women were treated in the Arab world and the Global South in general?

I've crossed the gates into the beautiful compound, but it's definitely not what it says in the brochure – and those who built its high walls are only just realising that.

When I moved to London to start a life with Ahmed, I had a whole load of mixed feelings. I knew I needed to move on, but I dreaded the separation from my mum and sister – the two constants and balancing agents of my life.

I quit two jobs that had made me financially independent to move to a new country and start from nothing. And of course, the small thing of being married and moving in with this man.

Yes, we knew each other for years but we didn't really *know* each other, not in the way you know someone when you've lived with them or shared a bed or a room with them – none of which we'd done because of course it wasn't allowed!

I was leaving everything and everyone I knew behind and walking into all sorts of unknowns. One thing I was sure of though: this was My Big Escape to the West – the promised land of freedom where I could finally be myself and no one would care what I looked like, what I wore or where I came from. The place where I could finally find my voice and be seen as me. I laugh as I write this now nearly fifteen years later.

To think that moving to the West was going to be the answer to all my problems ... that I was going to finally be Free with a big fat capital F. Just so naïve!

# 28.

# SHELLEY

Through the bumpy glass door, figures appeared outside as shadows – skinny, stark, ghostlike. The knuckles were large and brown.

A knock in the middle of the day in Doha. And a brown fist.

I asked Paul to go to the door.

A Pakistani man stood there, wringing his hands.

'You are the neighbours of Mr Simpson,' he said.

I stood between the living room and the hallway, my toes curling into the green carpet, observing the way the man's eyes shifted uneasily from left to right.

Yes. The Simpsons, our only nearby English-speaking neighbours, had recently moved to Qatar from Bahrain.

Jim and Karyn taught in the English language unit. Their daughters Haley and Charley were teenagers and had grown up in the Middle East. Jim and Karyn had done Oman, Bahrain, Dubai, Abu Dhabi – as teachers of English – moving away from each place when 'things got too much'. Qatar was the last stop.

Sometimes we would have tea together.

Sometimes the girls came over to our apartment to chat. Especially Haley.

The Pakistani man wrung his hands.

'I want that you ask Mr Simpson for forgiveness. If he can understand and forgive me. If he can do this, I will not be sentenced for forty lashes and deportation to Pakistan. My family, my wife … they depend on me.'

He was tearful.

What on earth could he have done that he needed Jim's forgiveness?

'Will you ask him, please, for me? I will come back tomorrow.'

Paul said he would talk to Jim, and the man could come back the next day. The terror in the man's eyes made my skin cold.

That afternoon, we went over to Jim and Karyn. The girls were there and the atmosphere in the house was subdued, as though a conversation had come to an abrupt halt as we entered.

Paul told them about the man.

Jim's face went crimson. The girls looked at their father.

'Forgive him? Forgive the man who tried to kidnap my children? Who drove them into the desert three nights ago? No way in hell!'

And then the girls told us they'd gone on Thursday night, Haley and Charley, as they often did, to the Shisha restaurant on the Corniche – a ten-minute taxi ride from Dafna. They'd done this often. The getting there and getting back was familiar to them. Doha was safe.

But on Thursday night, when they got the taxi back, they were followed by a Qatari man in a white Landcruiser who was talking on his phone in Arabic to the Pakistani taxi driver. Haley and Charley did not understand all the words, but a few alerted them to the fact that something was amiss. The next minute the taxi driver drove right off the road into the desert, followed by the Landcruiser. And Charlie and Haley, knowing the Middle East, became a storm of screaming and yelling and shouting threats at the taxi driver. They said he was surprised, taken off guard, stunned at the violence and agency of these young girls.

'You never think it will happen, but when it does, you know exactly what's going on and what you have to do,' Haley said, calm, as if her father and mother carried the full weight of the attempted kidnapping.

I listened, holding my breath.

'Yeah, so he relented and ignored the boss and drove us back to the apartments. And dad called the police.'

'He's going to get his forty lashes and be deported,' Jim says. 'He was going to kidnap my kids. No way in hell will I pardon him.'

And the guy in the Landcruiser?

Vanished.

We went back to our apartment after tea.

I put Tim down for his nap.

The next afternoon at the same time, the knock on the door.

I went into the bedroom.

I heard Paul's low tones. I imagined him saying, no, Mr Simpson will not forgive you for the attempted kidnapping of his daughters, even if you were doing this under orders.

And so, the potential kidnapper walked away from our apartment.

From the moment he was told to undertake the kidnapping, that taxi driver was doomed. There was no escape from hell for him. He may have been in the employ of the man in the white Landcruiser. At any rate, he was acting at the behest of this man, who was rich and powerful. The taxi driver was under duress. He would not have undertaken to try to kidnap these girls on his own, because of his low social status and the certainty that he would have been caught and punished. He chose to do what at first appeared to him to be the easier, safer option for him, and followed the command of his superior.

But then he did not expect this: the girls were aggressive and they threatened him and he must have contemplated the repercussions of kidnapping the daughters of a well-connected university professor. He grew frightened. Going through with the kidnapping could result in a death sentence. So, he turned the taxi around in the dust and took the girls home and hoped he could at least beg for forgiveness.

Who knows where the owner of the Landcruiser went after that? For sure, nothing would happen to him. He could have just roared off to find another to do a similar bidding.

Haley and Charley stopped taking taxis anywhere on their own.

I used to take a one-minute taxi to the Sheraton with Tim on afternoons when Paul was working. I stopped doing that.

The conscripted kidnapper was lashed forty times and deported to Pakistan.

I railed against where I found myself and I knew it was like trying to dam a river, trying to go against the geography aiding its tumbling to the sea.

Can we erase who we are, write ourselves beyond it?

I run to writing, make myself, out of my words, a compound. Here I can be with you, and we can be loud and obnoxious and Jewish and Muslim and we can talk about all the horrible and terrible things and name them and push back against colonialism and the Big Bad Patriarch – but while we do this, we know that we write into a space where Ghalia's poems might be. Poems that will never be written. Allow here, some white space and the title: *Ghalia's poems, and other unwritten stories.*

I write to escape the confines of my gender, my Jewish history, my female skin, even while I'm compelled to listen to the stories in my blood.

'I want to get out of Qatar,' I said to Paul after the taxi driver. 'We're in the middle of another contract. Do we have to run away?'

# 29.

# SHAIMAA

The thing that distinguished Doha for me from the get-go was how safe I felt ... until I didn't.

No pickpockets on public transport. Of course, no one mentioned that there was no public transport.

No harassment on the street. Except people failed to mention that harassment happened in luxurious cars and that the pests followed you home, tormented you all the way, put your life in danger just for laughs or to throw a small paper with a fucking phone number at you.

The very first time I got followed and harassed in a shop in Doha, I didn't understand what the hell was going on. Some man in a white thobe followed me and all I could hear were a bunch of numbers, I knew I was being sexually harassed because of the way he looked at me, and his disgustingly suggestive voice.

'It's his phone number!' my sister laughed.

'What? Why?'

'That's how they do it here. They whisper their phone numbers and if you're interested you give them a call.'

'And that works.'

'Apparently it does.'

Phone numbers. Sleazy invitations into more sleaziness and these were the harmless ones. The ones that didn't want to kidnap you or follow you up the stairs or throw things at your window to let you know they know where you live.

The number-whisperers were in many ways the benign harassers, if such an oxymoron could exist. And of course, there are the many other incidents we never hear about. The raped maids, the abandoned babies, the forced marriages.

It's all relative of course. And yes, there's no way I can for example compare the level or frequency of sexual harassment I've experienced in Egypt with that I have in Qatar. And yet as a woman, I've felt unsafe in both. Every day was open season.

*

I was trying to put my hands on the reasons I find it so easy and enjoyable to speak with you, my dearest Shell. How I can navigate the darkest places inside me with an unusual confidence and an almost dangerous lack of fear, knowing that you're the recipient.

It's been tricky trying to pin down why I, who's always had a problem finding the exact word for an exact thought at an exact moment, can speak with such ease and sometimes, dare I say precision, when I'm with you.

My words and my thoughts seem to find a way to each other and then to me. They are unburdened by how they might sound and whether they make sense.

I realise now that your greatest gift to me, other than being my TARDIS to a different world, is being the holder of my words. You have given me the gift of a loving audience. You have allowed a space for my thoughts to make their way into the world, surrounding them with the safety of an unjudgmental listener, more crucially an interested one. Someone who, for reasons still unknown to me, has decided to attach value to my words. To my story.

I think of all the girls you've taught, of all the women I knew and still know. The women whose ideas and opinions have been ignored and talked over at best and deliberately and violently stifled at worst. I've known many of those women. Shared classrooms with them when we were students. I've seen how for many of them education was their way out. Out of a house they were suck in most of the time. Out of a lifestyle and a way of thinking they were tethered to. I saw how many of them looked at you. With awe and intrigue. They would chat to you after class. They wanted to learn about your life but mainly they wanted you to see them and hear their words and you did fully and whole heartedly!

\*

Words are a dangerous business in my region. They're the space between who you are or want to be and who you pretend to be to get by in a society that allows little space for individual self-expression. Especially for women.

Words are a way to hold on to forbidden thoughts. They're the first promise of the fulfilment of ideas – on many occasions, they're the shapers of secret identities.

For me, they're the most basic and essential means to run away – perhaps that's why they're seen as dangerous.

Words are the vehicle of the voice so many women have been trying to find. But when a society decides that a group of people should be voiceless, then words become the enemy.

They become the difference between life and death.

Ironically, I don't have the right words to tell you how valuable and, frankly, lifesaving it is to have found that place of safety. I cherish and value that and don't take it for granted.

The darkness of shame seems to lift when you're around and all that is left are my words and me.

For that I can never repay you.

*

I struggle a lot with my voice – and yes, it's ironic because it's the tool I use the most in my profession. Truth is, I struggle to use it for anything other than my profession. My bread and butter is to tell stories, but when it comes to my own, the words elude me. It's like they've been in the shade inside me for so long and coming out to the light hurts and scares them, so they withdraw.

Mostly I feel like my story (which I have yet to figure out) has no place among the extraordinary stories I get to tell in my work. The ones of REAL struggle and REAL heroes and survivors. My work is best done with fewer words, with less of my voice and more of the voice of others. My work is NOT about me. I tell stories of others. Mine is irrelevant. 'You are not the story.' All our journalism teachers would tell us. 'Never make it about you.'

And yet sometimes, after a long and emotionally exhausting day, I wonder how I can separate myself from all of it.

How do I stop hearing a mother's wail as she sits next to the corpse of her teenage son who is being readied for burial after a school massacre in Peshawar? How do I calm my body when it shudders at the thought of being surrounded by a mob as I report in the village of Asia Bibi, the Pakistani Christian woman who was accused of blasphemy and had a price on her head even when she was in prison? What would've happened if the police didn't arrive in time?

'You know that cafe in Baghdad we filmed in last week?' My producer once told me after an exhausting trip to Iraq.

'Yeah, what about it?' I'd said wearily.

'Bombed,' he said. 'Oh, and that great guy who was our fixer in Libya? Killed.'

I nod. I move on.

This job that I love and do is an absolute privilege. But sometimes I have to stifle so much to get through it. Mostly my own voice – even though it's the most valuable thing I possess.

I fought tooth and nail for my voice. I fought for it in the place I ran away from and I fought and I'm still fighting for it in all the places I've run to.

# 30.

# SHELLEY

Shaimaa, your story is as necessary to being you in the world as breath to life.

After running away so often, taking on different selves, I feel the shards of a disparate, geographically dislocated self re-forming. But it means going into the wounds.

I did not know how we would ever leave. The world seemed to have moved on without us, Paul and me, and there seemed to be no place, no way to earn a living outside of Doha, as if the only thing of value we had to offer was our English, our words.

I tried to write.

I was unable to produce anything but the children's stories I was writing. I had lost my adult voice. It felt as though it had been blacked out.

But without this job in Qatar I had no other way of making money.

Also, without Paul in his job in Qatar I had no way of having my job in Qatar.

My position as an earner of any kind was contingent upon being with him, out of South Africa, employed by his employer.

Just before Paul and I got married and left South Africa, he wrote me a story. It was a fairytale written in a small black book with lined pages. He painted the black cover with blue and yellow and red and green and white acrylic. On the first page, written in big chunky ballpoint pen letters: *The Adventures of Shelley and Paul.*

The story was about two characters who set off on a wild adventure. It was funny and sweet – illustrated in ballpoint pen. The adventurers may have faced enormous obstacles, but they never lost their sense of humour and they were there for each other. They inscribed their dreams of what they wanted to do into the universe, and in the story, the universe heard. With our story in my pocket, I felt safe. With such a story, we were never going to be a cliché. We would be curious and alive and love the world and the world would love us back. Never would we fall into being a boring husband/wife unit, where a husband might speak and a wife would finish or devour his sentence before it was even out of his mouth – or where the distance between them might grow until they no longer spoke the same language or remembered the shared dream they once tried to inscribe into the universe.

We didn't wear wedding rings – we gave each other quartz crystals dug from a mountainside in Cape Town where I'd spent my childhood. We were the characters in a story of our own making.

When we left London for Qatar after all our failed job applications, we were held aloft by our story.

In the green-carpeted apartment after teaching all day in different shifts, Paul made us dinner. I fed Tim. I realised that it had been some time since I last thought about money and whether we had enough. We had arrived at a coveted position: we were one of those couples who had enough money to live on and not worry. Not riches or wealth, but an income that more than covered our needs.

What right did I have to be ungrateful for this, to want to leave?

I could never leave anyway.

We looked out at the rubble of the fallen building.

And I wondered ... what happened to our story – a story that once felt as full of potential as the universe and that suddenly seemed to have nowhere to go?

Did he still love me or not love me, I asked him. Which one was true?

He loved me – underneath, he said.

That night he went out to play lead guitar in the *Little Shop of Horrors* musical put on by the Doha Players. Tim was asleep and the phone rang.

'Mrs Shelley, how are you? It's Layla.'

She was a colleague I didn't know very well, though we always nodded and said hello. Layla was shy and quiet, a member of a local wealthy family. Our mailboxes were next to one another.

'Very well and you?' How did she get my number? I didn't ask.

'Yes, good. I was wondering if you might have some time to talk to me about a question I have.'

'Sure,' I said. 'We can talk now if you like?'

'I'd prefer if I might come to your apartment. Would that suit you?'

'Yes,' I said. 'Paul will be home so I won't be alone,' I said, knowing that she might not want to come over if she knew there was a man in the house.

'That doesn't matter,' she said. 'I can talk to you both. You live in Dafna?'

'Yes,' I said.

We arranged to meet the following afternoon.

*

I stood on the balcony of the Dafna apartments and looked at the road signs in Arabic, heard the late afternoon call to prayer. A woman wrapped in her abaya walked across the desert towards us, looking left and right over her shoulder. Paul was looking after Tim and I went to open the door when I heard the soft knock.

Layla, English professor, was about thirty-two. She was beautiful as she walked down the passage and swirled out of her abaya. Black boots, tight jeans, a black cotton jacket and white shirt. She wore gold bracelets and a necklace, had short dark hair and a face that could have graced the covers of any *Vogue* magazine. She went into the living room and sat on the couch. I made us tea.

'I would like to ask for your thoughts on something,' she said.

'Sure,' I said.

'I can trust you.' This wasn't a question.

She sipped her tea. 'In Qatar it's not common to be a divorced woman,' she said. 'I am a divorced woman with a fifteen-year-old daughter. You've read the book *Not Without my Daughter*?'

'I've heard of it. I know the story.'

'Similar story to mine.'

'Oh.'

'Well, I lived in London where I did my PhD, and since then, all I've dreamt of is to go back. I have been trying to leave Qatar for seven years. My ex-husband – he says I can go, but not take my daughter. So, maybe you can help.' She looked around the apartment. 'They tap the phones,' she said. 'That was why I had to come here.'

'Can't you just go on a holiday and not come back?' I asked.

She put her finger to her lips indicating I should speak more quietly. What, I thought, the place can't be bugged?

'I can leave,' she said, 'but my ex-husband will not let my daughter come with me.'

I remembered what you said, Shaimaa, about fathers owning their children.

'I need your help on this matter.' And then softly. 'I have a plan to run away – but it carries a great risk and I need to be clever.'

Her aquiline features were sharp and pronounced. Beneath the beauty, a warrior disposition, someone willing to risk everything.

'What can I do?' Did she know about Reza? I felt nervous.

'I can't book a ticket to England or get a visa to England to go with my daughter. Everyone will stop me because they know I would like to go. I can't use my internet because everything I do is observed and monitored and what I look at is not a secret from my ex-husband and his many connections. Can you do some research for me? Is there a way that I could, perhaps, travel to France, and from there, get a visa to England? If I go on holiday to France with my daughter, no one will worry me. They know I do not want to live in France.'

'I'll do some research and let you know,' I said.

'Thank you.'

She finished her tea and stood up.

She swept her abaya around her. The *Vogue* model vanished. She slipped out of our door.

I watched her slender figure shimmering in the heat as she walked away from Dafna and disappeared into the dust. She must have parked some distance from the apartment.

That evening, Paul and I set to work side-by-side at the computer.

'Do you think it's safe for us to look these things up?'

'I think so,' he said.

*

I called her the next day.

'I have something for you,' I said.

'Shh,' she said. 'I'd prefer nothing over the phone. I will come to you in the afternoon,' she said.

She arrived again, an anonymous someone at the door, and came into the living room, shedding her disguise and emerging from the shadow that slipped down onto the couch. 'Tell me,' she said. I handed her a piece of paper.

'With a Qatari passport, it looks like you can get a Schengen visa. The visa allows you into the Schengen states in Europe. From France you can apply for a UK visa, for example, or you could go into the UK in transit for forty-eight hours, and if you needed to, claim asylum.'

'UK is not listed on this Schengen visa?'

'No.'

She smiled. 'Thank you.'

When she said goodbye to me and to Paul that afternoon, she gave us each a hug. 'Thank you for that. I hope I don't see you again.'

I felt tearful as she disappeared back into her abaya, then out of the door and later, across the dusty space between Dafna and where she parked her car.

*

After a holiday break, we went back to work. Layla's mailbox filled with unopened letters. It filled to bursting and then the letters spilled onto the floor. Her office door remained locked. Nobody said a word.

One day, her mailbox was empty; the name sign on her office door was removed. Layla vanished. Without even a breath of wind or a single word to mark her exit she was gone from the English department, from the country, as if she had never existed.

Were we, I wondered, the facilitators of runaways?

I hope and imagine that Layla and her daughter found their way to England and are living there happily somewhere still today.

*

Paul came home after midnight.

He reached out to touch me. I turned away from him and lay there, staring into the darkness.

*

In that harsh place where love was struggling to keep its colour, where sleep was scarce, where the bulldozers began cleaning up the rubble left behind by the fallen buildings outside Dafna, where a Pakistani man was flogged and deported after attempting to kidnap our neighbour's daughters at the behest of his boss, I started to think seriously of my own escape.

Me, and how many others?

With at least one First World passport (Paul's) between us, we could find a way to get out of the Middle East, but I wasn't so sure how, both practically and economically. When we first arrived in Doha, we had 300 pounds in the whole world left. After three years, we had saved around 70,000 American dollars. How long could we live on that before we were again close to the ground? There was no safety net in South Africa. No dole. I'd lost my residence in the UK because we'd moved to Qatar, though Paul could return – but job prospects had been bleak three years before and they didn't look to be any better.

Paul was in the middle of a second two-year teaching contract.

The beauty of these contracts: apparently they could be broken by the university, but not by the employee.

The newspaper was full of notices about those 'absconding' – leaving without fulfilling their contracts. I could not imagine the punishments.

But each day, I drew strength from teaching on the women's side.

We wrote poetry and I felt increasingly anxious about that. Were we doing something transgressive? I ensured that towards the end of the lesson we went back to *Ship or Sheep* in case Dr Johara, the latest monitor of the corridor and classrooms, decided to terrorise us by peering accusingly through the small window into the class.

'Your poems are so full of life,' I said. 'They wouldn't be out of place in Keats's time, I promise you.'

After class, Wafaa, using crutches as she had since I'd first met her, hobbled towards me. 'Mrs Shelley I love you,' she said. 'You and Mr Paul. I love both of you.'

'That's a very sweet thing to say, Wafaa.'

Paul taught literature on the women's side, and many of the students were in my class and in his. I smiled.

She reached into her bag with its gold chain and pulled out a gift. 'For you and Mr Paul.' She grinned. I held the wrapped gift in my hand. 'What is it?'

'Two gold watches from the souk,' she said.

'Wow,' I said. It was two weeks to go until the end of semester exams. 'That's so kind of you,' I said. 'But I tell you what. Why don't you hold onto the gifts until the end of term – after exams, and then you can give them to me? I'd feel so much happier if you did that.'

I didn't want to hurt her. But I didn't want to be bribed, or to be seen to be bribable.

'All right,' she said, and took back the gifts, looking less cheerful.

'Wafaa, you're a very good student. You've worked really hard. I don't think you'll have any problem getting through the exams.'

A flicker of fear in her eyes and she shifted on her crutches.

She smiled. Her mouth was full of so many teeth I found myself trying to count them. The way she leaned – like a gnarled tree battered by wind until it grew askew.

It looked as though she was in pain.

'I wanted to ask you, Wafaa, are you okay? Were you in an accident?'

'No. No accident.'

'Oh. What happened?'

'I was born like this. It happens. My mother is my father's first wife. She's also his first cousin. So, I have double the teeth that you have. Also, look,' she showed me her arms. They were twisted. Her thumbs pointed to the ground when her hands were relaxed, she explained. Because, she said, 'I have two ulnas, and two radiuses. That's me,' she said. 'My sisters don't have this because they're from my father's second wife and she's not his cousin. It's all right, Mrs Shelley,' she said. 'Don't look worried. God made me this way. It's nothing to be sad about.'

'No, of course not. You're right Wafaa.'

'Thank you. I enjoyed the poetry. I will bring the gifts back at the end. After the exams.'

'Thanks, Wafaa. You're very kind and I'll look forward to that.'

Nayrouz came up to me. She was about my age, and heavily pregnant. 'I feel sorry for her,' she said. 'It's unlikely she'll ever be married. Or experience the fulfilment of motherhood.'

'She's a lovely person,' I said. 'I'm sure she'll have a happy life.'

Nayrouz laughed without humour. 'Me and you both. We wish that,' she said. 'But we know that's not true.'

I took a deep breath. 'When are you due?'

'Tomorrow,' she said. 'But I think I'm in labour, so I'm sorry but I need to go and call my driver.'

'Oh, goodness!'

'Not a big deal, Mrs Shelley. Western women make such a big fuss about birth. It's just another thing we have to do here. And my husband works at the hospital. So I'm one of the lucky ones. He'll be able to be there with me. Maybe give me some drugs.'

'Oh, you can get drugs? Like an epidural?'

'Can't depend on it. But I'm hoping. He knows people high up. I think I should hurry.'

'Go! Go! I hope it goes well,' I said. 'Good luck with everything.'

'I'll try to make it back for the exam.'

I watched her walk away holding her stomach. I pitied anyone who had to face childbirth.

If you knew someone high up, you might get pain relief. If your husband worked at the hospital, he might be present for the birth of his child. I was relieved for Nayrouz. But for the most part, I worried about the others: teenage girls were left to the agonies of childbirth and were at the mercy of whomever presided over them.

*

At the end of the semester, I went home with heart-shaped balloons and cards and flowers. I loved these young women. They shared their stories with me. Their hopes and dreams.

Jamila confessed she was terrified of getting married.

Latifa said in her fantasies she met a handsome and kind British man in England. He promised she would be his only wife.

The mosaic of my life in Qatar was tinged with desert orange, but there were other colours, and when I thought of leaving them, I saw no easy way of letting go.

*

One afternoon I was at the Sheraton Hotel with Tim. Paul was at work. I was pushing Tim in his pram in front of a swinging glass door, when a Qatari man, deep in conversation with another, pushed through the door. He knocked Tim's pram over and sent my baby sprawling onto the floor. I rushed to pick Tim up. He was crying. I was crying. Furious. Who was this idiot who had knocked my precious son to the ground?

I held myself together. I was afraid of further upsetting Tim.

'I'm sorry,' said the man. 'Is your baby okay?'

'Yes,' I said. No, I meant, can't you see?

The next day, Paul and Tim and I were sitting on the grass. It was forty degrees Celsius and the sun was going down and the sky turned purple over the Arabian Gulf. Tim was crawling across the ground when a man in a thobe approached us.

He ignored me. The Glass-Door-Patriarch who had knocked my baby from his pram.

'Is this your baby?' he said to Paul.

'Yes.'

The man opened his wallet. He pulled out a gold-embossed business card. He handed it to Paul. 'If you ever need anything, call me.'

Paul took the card, bewildered.

After the man left, we read the card, looked at one another.

Mohammed Bin – Someone. Head of the CID. The Secret Police.

I had nearly told the head of the Secret Police to fuck off.

'If you don't get me out of here soon,' I said to Paul, 'I'm going to do something crazy to one of these men and get us into trouble and you might find yourself trying to get me out of a Qatari jail. I just want a normal life.'

*

Paul applied for hundreds of jobs all over the world.

I applied for residence in New Zealand.

I got it.

We had no jobs, but, I thought, there's a country with a decent social system. I wanted to go.

Paul didn't think that going to New Zealand to be unemployed was a smart move.

I didn't want to stay in Qatar.

And then after we had booked flights to Auckland and put down a deposit on a house to rent and hired a car and imagined throwing ourselves again across the world with nothing, Paul received an offer to teach at a small community college in Pendleton, Oregon.

'If we go to New Zealand, we'll be poor,' Paul said.

'If we go to America, we won't have residence and I won't be able to work and we'll have to pay lawyers thousands and thousands of dollars to get a Green Card.'

'I wrote to all the universities in New Zealand and one of the professors in Waikato wrote back and said the job market for academics there is so tough that even if one of them dies there won't be a position for me. At least he wrote back,' he said. 'And now here's a real job offer in a First World country.'

I looked up Pendleton, Oregon.

It was in the high desert.

It had about seventeen or was it a hundred churches.

And a woollen mill.

And an annual rodeo.

It was the First World.

With a heavy heart I cancelled everything to and in New Zealand.

Residence in a place without a job vs a job in a place without residence.

The answer as to where we had to go was obvious.

And now we had to plan how to leave.

*

You came with us to the Sheraton club and we sat there on the grass on a mound, and I thought I should tell you that I was Jewish. That I came from a long line that stretched back into the mists of time, of Jewish refugees, and before then, back to Abraham. Both Islam and Judaism are seen as Abrahamic religions and I understand that the practice of Islam, the basis of its religious practice, and its structure is influenced by Judaism; that back in time, under the Constitution of Medina, the Rabbi Mukhayriq pledged all his wealth to the prophet Mohammed in the event of his death, and the prophet called the Rabbi 'the best of Jews'. There was early inter-faith harmony – but it didn't last. The Jewish people violated the Constitution of Medina, 700 Jews were executed and war ensued – well, that's a simple version of the story. But here we are, children of these tribes, these religions.

As we write ourselves together, I know I want to escape what the world wants to impose on us – that we are at war, that the families and ancestors and cousins who stand behind us, perhaps fight one another, demonise one another, divide the world down the middle.

# 31.

# SHAIMAA

'So you know, I'm Jewish,' you said as you and Paul and I sat on the grass in the Sheraton one day.

I remember you looked at the sky when you said that. And I was looking at the water. Paul didn't say much.

And I said 'Oh. Okay.' And that was that. I think you said something about not sharing this or not repeating it which of course I didn't and wouldn't have.

'This should change something, right?' I asked myself. 'Yeah, but it doesn't. Why should it?' I had no answers.

All I knew was that this was a profound piece of information you shared with me about your heritage and yet it changed nothing about how I felt about you or about our friendship.

Your last few months in Doha felt like living in a pressure cooker. Every day, it felt to me, something or someone added to that heaviness and it just kept weighing you down! I wonder Shell, before the heaviness set in, did you enjoy your time in Doha? There were many difficulties of course, but looking back after all those decades, what did you like about it? What memories did that place leave with you? I have many – so many! Even though I knew when I left that it was the right time to go.

\*

I believe you witnessed that miracle in Layla, your beautiful friend who escaped with her daughter. I can only imagine the fear. The absolute terror she was living in within the gates of what I'm sure was a stunning palace of a home in Doha.

To sit and contemplate that escape. To think of the consequences for her and her daughter and yet to know that survival for them both meant running away … To know what could've happened to her and to have done it anyway, is a kind of courage that I simply don't have or know much about but I stand in awe of.

I do know however, that she could've never ever done that by confronting the system or by asking questions or by demanding that her life and liberties be acknowledged. She got over the system by going around it, by imagining a better life – a more real life for herself and her daughter and then having the courage to turn imagination into a plan.

Imagination, for many, is where hopes and dreams live. For women under oppressive regimes, imagination is where reality is tolerated and plans are made.

It's a lifeline.

I know that my biggest plans and ambitions started with imagination. Imagination says, 'Hey! There's something different. Things could be different. You could be different.'

Maybe when your student told you about her fantasy of the British blind man whom she marries and brings back to Doha with her, it was her imagining a life that was full of love. She imagined being loved for herself, being loved differently. She imagined she was someone's choice not someone's other end of an arranged marriage. She imagined a life where her partner wanted her as an individual not as an auxiliary of a father or a brother. She imagined she was her own person and that she decided to be with someone.

Imagination has always been my trusted fortress. This is where we see ourselves fully flourish.

It's no surprise that dictators find thinkers, artists, academics, books and education so threatening. These are the sources of ideas and imagination.

To me the most dangerous thing for a woman is not about something or someone limiting where she can go and what she can wear. The most dangerous thing is when something or someone limits her thoughts – her ability to imagine, her ability to express herself even to herself, her capacity to articulate something in her mind further and deeper than what is permitted.

My paternal grandmother was an illiterate woman – she lived a comfortable if tense and confined life with her five children and husband. She's one of my biggest heroes – a role model that I've always loved and looked up to in awe. A study in survival, open-mindedness and a vivid imagination.

I believe what carried Grandma through the years wasn't just her grit and her lack of options. I am convinced that her perseverance had a lot to do with her imagination.

What she lacked in formal education, I feel, she made up for in her commitment to her kids and in a home she made so beautiful and welcoming.

My grandmother could turn anything into a work of art. She could make anything beautiful. Every corner of her home reflected that.

She loved sunlight and insisted on open windows – 'light and air have to enter the home every day,' she'd say. I got that from her, I'm positive.

She was adamant about beautiful surroundings. She loved trying new things.

Why would a woman of a generation so entrenched in tradition and of doing things the same way always be so open to new things? She loved to try new recipes; she'd change the décor of her home every few months; when she could she loved to go out, to see things and people.

When she couldn't get something to work, like a new phone, or a new blender she would ask us grandchildren to read the instructions and in our boredom, when we'd try to just do it so we could go play, she'd say, 'No! Don't do it for me! Teach me how to do it ...'

Although my grandfather was the one with the exciting military stories, the one who travelled, the one who knew places and people, to me, she was easily the more interesting of the two.

*

My mother always said that if my grandmother had learned to read and was given chance at an education, she would've been one of the first female government ministers in Egypt. In her very limited world, I believe my grandmother had unlimited ideas of who she was and what she could've become. I got that from her, I have no doubt. Imagination hasn't only been my go-to place, it's been my saviour!

I'd say to myself. 'They can tell me what I can and can't do in life, they can tell me I'm not smart enough, good enough, pious enough, woman enough ... but they can't touch me in here. They can't touch my imagination.'

Some of it though ... I mean, the life where my imaginary self speaks seven languages and goes on to be an Oscar-winning actress and filmmaker and has all these celebs fall in love with her – that lives only and happily in my mind, is there for my personal pleasure and consumption.

But the part where I imagine something different for myself, something more profound, meaningful ... the part where I imagine myself whole, fearless, free … the part where I imagine escaping the confines of fear … not my super human self, but my 'why not' self … my 'I-know-that-you-can't-but-you-can-try' self … my 'show-'em' self: these selves have saved me – these selves have surrounded me and carried me through when I was convinced things were out of bounds and impossible for someone like me. These selves live in my imagination.

*

Recently, my real barometer as to when I'm in my 'dark place' has been when I can't access my imagination. That's when I begin to really worry.

The very act of running away is, in its essence, an act of imagination. To get out you have to imagine yourself out – of a place, of a situation.

Then the work begins to move – which in our region is very difficult and nigh on impossible if you're a woman on your own.

Before I left Egypt for Qatar, Qatar for the UK, the UK for Pakistan, then Australia and all the countries in between, I know that I had a vivid picture in my head of saying goodbye to people and a vivid sense that I was the one 'who leaves'. You can argue that psychologically this was my brain trying to manage my incredible frustration with my limitations and my sense of confinement as a young woman.

*

I don't need to imagine, however, why you wanted to leave. Paul seemed to be thriving in this new environment and you weren't. You didn't need to worry about money, but it sounds to me like you started worrying about your very being, about where you belonged while the man you loved was making his way comfortably in the life of superficial safety of Doha and you were having to deal with small and not so small daily frustrations.

\*

*A resident in a country with no job.*

*A job in a country with no residence.*

This is so precisely and piercingly the story of mine and many other diaspora families' existence – especially in the Gulf.

Many traded the permanence of homelands with no prospects for the transience and the riches of the Gulf.

Many made a living and lost real life. Many promised that the following year was going to be the last before they headed home. But many were too distracted to realise that home had faded away and what was left were their memories of it.

Many chose to spend their lives in financial exile. Others who go back by choice or are forced to leave the makeshift Oasis confront a homeland that has moved on without them and where they have no real place. They face the fact that they've become perpetual strangers.

It's a well-trodden transaction.

Come to country. Work. Get paid. Leave.

No labour rights. No residency. No sense of belonging.

\*

And yet, so many monumental moments in my life happened in Doha. I spent my first ten adult years in Doha, from sixteen to twenty-six. I met my husband in Doha. I had my first job in broadcast in Doha. I shared beautiful moments with the best of friends there.

I learned to drive and had my first car accident there. My first real academic achievement was in Doha. My first pay cheque was in Doha and yet for all those seminal moments, I knew and was reminded every day that this was not my home.

I could never fully soften into my existence in Qatar. I knew that any life I wanted to build there was a sandcastle that could be washed away when someone at the university decided they didn't need my mother's services anymore.

This unsteadiness – to me – is a subtle type of violence. When you can't fully relax into being – when you know the shadow of financial hardship is hanging over you – when you know that you need more than you are needed.

For me, there was always the fear of going back to my small life in Alexandria. While I had fond childhood memories, home was a place to escape not a destination to long for.

I never really understood those who longed for home. Not as an idea or the nostalgia for days long gone, but actually being home. Immersing themselves in it again. In its reality and frustrations. Home to me was always a suffocating notion, a reminder that while many things have changed in my life, nothing really had changed inside me when I was at home. A reminder that my only real home was my imagination.

# 32.

# SHELLEY

In writing there is always an undoing. Also, a remaking. You let air flow through my narrative, stop stories from turning to stone. I like to believe we can always redraft even when we think a version of things is hard frozen.

I wish I'd met your grandmother. She sounds like an extraordinary woman. Your seeing her and describing her liberates her so I and others might see her, appreciate her. You write her and she appears in my imagination unfettered, a free human being.

If there are no words with which to write a Self out of darkness, I can't imagine the pain.

*

How to escape:

1. Have at least one First World passport in your family.
2. Speak a version of fluent English that the Big Bad Patriarch would approve of.
3. Be subservient no matter what.

4.   Have some money.

5.   Have somewhere to go.

If you don't check all five boxes things are going to be very, very difficult.

Paul and I had a First World passport between us.

But that created a power imbalance. If our relationship crumbled, I had nowhere to go except back to my parents in South Africa.

Heartbreak at losing love in the desert carried with it a panic of being deserted, of tumbling back to where I came from. Hitting the big snake in the Snakes & Ladders game on ninety-seven that sends you all the way back down to the bottom row.

In theory I was much better off than my young students. I could leave. I spoke Received Pronunciation English – the equivalent of having a secret membership to a secret club when it comes to being a runaway. I might feel like a refugee, but I was in excellent disguise. I could take shelter behind Received Pronunciation English and no one would ever be able to see my desperation, even when I was 300 pounds from having nothing in the world. I could hide my fear of inheriting the legacy of generations of Ashkenazi Jews fleeing persecution – a fear that there was a program in my DNA to end up somewhere, sometime, at the unfortunate end of anti-Semitism. I could be a First World person as I planned my escape. I knew though, even in my desperation to leave, that I would think back with nostalgia about my women students – about the relationships that were so pure. I knew I would miss the upside down moon in a lilac sky. I would miss you. Elements of Qatar would haunt me with their strange beauty regardless of my struggles.

\*

I'm in awe of your courage with words. I forget that you write in English and grew up speaking Arabic. You wear English like it's your own skin. I don't know what that's like for you. I speak German fluently and apparently without an accent; it takes people a while to figure out I'm not German, and don't have German parents – only Yiddish great-grandparents. And yet when I speak German, I feel like I'm casting an avatar out into the world. She looks like me, but she has a different disposition. She knows how to say 'es ist mir Sheißegal,' or 'es ist echt gemütlich' and mean it wholeheartedly, even when there are no direct translations. But I hover in that second language, a ghost behind the German words. The person people take me for in the German translation of myself is a construct. I am not her. I create her and almost merge with her. But you swim in English like it's your mother tongue, translating a world, becoming my Rosetta Stone into that world, allowing me to learn and decode and understand what otherwise would have been as out of reach as a distant galaxy. Words are everything. Your English words are a gateway through which I step into a world that would not otherwise have even a sliver of an entry point for someone like me. In this world, I can stand there and hear the heart of Bassel, the Palestinian boy; I can listen to the stories of my students, and feel their lives, and learn what they are bound by, and understand the gradations of suppression and oppression that play out in that world. And I can see how we are positioned by geography, ethnicity, religion, regardless of how much we push against this.

*

I left South Africa for many reasons and this was one of them: just before the end of apartheid a close friend of ours, Sam Mabe, a prominent black journalist, began writing about education and freedom and his hopeful and idealistic vision of a multi-racial transformed future South Africa. He eloquently turned anger and despair to hope and allowed white readers to read on a daily basis, this black man's forgiving and fiercely intelligent view of his country.

One day, Sam came home from work to his house in a township. As he was approaching his gate, someone called his name. He turned to see who it was.

He was shot dead at point blank range. The killers were members of the military wing of the right-wing government. They wanted him quiet.

I had just won my first literary award. I was writing about similar things as a young adult – about hope for South Africa, and freedom – and I was already living a tangled multi-racial life. And then this man died for his words.

I know this was naïve, because on every landmass people are being killed for their words, but I did not want to live in a place where writers could die for their words. Where Sam died for his words.

So, this is why what you do fills me with admiration and vicarious dread. I ran away from everything you ran towards. You reported from Egypt during the Arab Spring and your name was all over the news when you were taken to prison in your own country. And then you were released. When you were in Pakistan, I was in awe of your courage. That you would go willingly into that very situation, where women's words of all things could put your life in danger. You stood in a courtroom in Pakistan a breath away from the father and husband who had murdered a young woman in a notorious honour killing. They knew you. They could have found you if they wanted to.

I would not have slept at night, fearing reprisals. How are you so brave?

*

I have taken more than twenty years and five continents to finally hide myself away in a semi-rural Queensland suburb where I forget to lock the doors at night, where some don't even lock, where there is nothing to remind me of what it feels like to drive home at night in South Africa and realise the back window of the car is broken and think that someone is in the car and any minute now I will be shot, or where every thunderstorm brings with it the fear of breaking glass and intruders with AK47s and there are no locks strong enough and no walls high enough to keep anyone safe. Where I don't fear the Secret Police tapping my conversations and fear that they could arrest me for doing an internet search for desperate women wanting to escape.

*

I hide from everything that you run towards. I admire your struggle to get the words right, to strip back the comfortable veneer and allow a space in which both of us can unravel cliché and upend our own versions of our lives and maybe dissolve hard and fast pictures of what it means to carry the legacy of being called *Muslim* or *Jew*.

I came to a point in Doha when I knew I, we, had to leave. I wanted to write more than children's stories. I wanted to wear sleeveless shirts and go on a date with Paul and eat together in public. Would the love that almost died in the desert be given a chance at new life if we could get out?

I convinced myself that any other kind of struggle would be worth it if I could just breathe the air of the First World on a daily basis.

*

Paul accepted the job in Oregon, in the USA, and I let go of the dream of New Zealand. I would go to America on an H2 visa: an H2 visa gives a person the status of a spouse of someone allowed to work. I would not be allowed to work myself, of course. Since I had a toddler, I thought, immigration officials on any side of the border would be quite satisfied with the idea that a woman would follow her husband to his new job in a new country and that she would have no problem staying at home and being a housewife and a mother to a two-year-old.

*

Every summer, most expats left Doha for a three-month holiday. The temperatures topped 57 degrees. The last few weeks before the end of semester of our third year in Qatar played themselves out in suffocating heat. I felt as though we were living in an oven.

Meanwhile, we had to be very quiet about our plans to go. I told only you. Even the man I worked with closely in the Language Lab at the university, whom I considered a friend, I did not tell. It was as if Reza and Layla provided me with the essential code of conduct for making an exit. It had to be as quiet as humanly possible. We got rid of only a few things, and booked our tickets to London, as if we were going away on holiday. From there, we planned to go to the US Embassy in London and get our visas for America.

We had nowhere to go to once we got to Oregon, but Paul's new colleague wrote to us just before we left and said we would be welcome to stay in their bunkhouse in Pendleton, which was comfy and which her mother and father had built to stay in. I looked up 'bunkhouse' on the internet, as I wasn't sure what it was. We would be welcome, Caroline said, to be there for as long as necessary. She seemed kind. She said she didn't know what it was like travelling that far across the world with a two-year-old, but she had no doubt it was challenging. I was so touched by the warmth she offered and the safe landing place she was providing for us to arrive to, I felt ready to go.

Then our internet cut out.

A message came through to Paul that he needed to go in to speak to an official at the university to sort out his internet connection.

Paul went in.

He spoke to the official. He was told just that there had been a problem, and now it was sorted out. The connection was back on again.

Paul came home desperately uneasy. 'I think our emails are being monitored. And this is their way of telling me.'

I wished we could teleport ourselves out of there.

My only sadness was leaving you.

I thought about my students and I knew that I would never have students like this again. There was a part of me that mourned the loss of this connection – this special kind of warmth that could only exist under these circumstances. Tim was almost two.

And then Paul went to the university to get his exit visa stamped into his passport. Without an exit visa, no employee could leave. I did not need a university exit visa because Paul was my owner and he could give me an exit visa. When Paul arrived at the university, the person responsible for giving out the exit visas was not there.

'He's gone,' said his assistant. 'Gone to France, coming back in August.'

'In August?' Paul was horrified. He thought they'd been monitoring our emails and now they were not going to let us go. 'What am I supposed to do? I have to go to England next week!'

The man said, 'All right, come here.' He unlocked the door to the office. He opened some drawers at the professor's big oak table. He rustled around and found a stamp. He asked for Paul's passport. He stamped it. And he handed it back to Paul and Paul, in shock, stammered, 'Thank you,' then stumbled out of the room and came home to tell me the story.

In the countdown to leaving I felt stomach-churning fear. I wished I could take you with me.

We packed our suitcases and apartment, but not too much. We left food in the fridge. Paul left his suit hanging in the cupboard. We left our books on the shelves. We took only what we could carry and we left $10,000 in our bank account, which we ultimately never retrieved. We sold our car and rented one. We made our plans, and we said goodbye.

And we gave you the key to our apartment. Anything you find that you might need, take it. Keep the key and don't let anyone know that you have it.

We drove it to the airport. At the airport I was sick with fear. I remembered all the articles about people absconding. We were doing exactly that: absconding, leaving, as if to go on holiday with nothing but two suitcases, doing a runner, as they said, because there was no way for us to break a contract.

When we came to customs, the official paged slowly and deliberately through our passports looking at every single item, reading each visa stamp, each page while the line built up behind us. He checked his computer, checked our passports checked his computer again, no doubt for names of people or suspects who might be doing a runner. And then suddenly, his pager went off. He looked at it and smiled and then looked up at us.

'Go, go,' he said, waving us through. Paul and I looked at each other. My legs were shaking as we went through. We sat in the waiting lounge. The flight was delayed by half an hour. Then, we finally boarded and sat down in our seats and the moments slowed until I could hardly stand to breath. I held Tim and he slept on me, his head sweaty against my chest. And then the announcement:

'The flight has been delayed because of some problems with some passengers.'

Paul and I looked at each other. All the blood went out of my face. Paul said, 'If they want me, you stay on the plane and you go to England with Tim.' He wrote a quick note giving me permission to leave the country without him. 'I'll deal with whatever.'

'No,' I said, 'No, I can't. I can't do that!' I was thinking about how I would be travelling to England as a South African with no job offer myself in America, and no residence in England and literally, nowhere to go. I felt desperate.

'You'll figure it out,' Paul said. 'You can't stay in Qatar if they put me in jail. You and Tim have to go.'

And then we waited. I imagined all the worst possible scenarios that anyone with an active imagination could. And then a few exhausted-looking Iraqi women finally boarded the plane and took their seats. The doors closed the overhead lockers were secured. And the captain announced that we would be departing shortly.

I almost couldn't believe it. The problem was not with us. The problem was with these passengers. Even right up until the moment that the plane wheels left the runway, I was terrified that we would be pulled back. I sat frozen for hours going through the motions of eating food, drinking, looking out the window. I thought, I don't even mind if we crash as long as we crash over Europe somewhere. Let me die in the First World. I didn't realise the level of stress that underpinned every word, every step, every breath. I didn't know what I was carrying until we were over France, and then I burst into tears because I realised we had left. We were going to be in England in one hour.

Two weeks after we did our runner, another colleague did the same. She was stopped at the airport. We heard she was arrested. She was imprisoned. She was made to pay back various amounts of money before she was released from prison and allowed out of the country.

In England we stayed with friends and relatives. We waited weeks for an appointment at the US Embassy to get our visas for America. Finally, the day came. We went to the window with our passports. They took my passport and looked at it. It had been stapled, written on, dog-eared and mangled by the Qatari government.

'I'm very sorry,' the immigration officer said. 'You're going to have to apply for a new passport. This one is significantly altered and therefore illegal.'

And so, getting to America took a month longer than anticipated. We stayed with people we knew and took Tim to parks and to the zoo for the first time, where he saw animals he'd never seen and ate ice cream he'd never tasted. It was summertime, and all the daisies were out. Tim had never seen daisies. He lay down on his back in the grass and ran his fingers over the tiny white flowers. 'Ma,' he said to me. 'These flowers are smiling.'

# 33.

# SHAIMAA

God, I can physically feel the horror, your stomach turning on itself. The trembling as you tried to keep yourself and your family together. The realisation of what little control you had at this moment must've been sickening.

I can't remember how I felt when you told me you were leaving. I remember that I wasn't surprised. It felt like the natural thing to happen. Even though, till the very last day, you were so kind and cheerful, I could sense how unhappy and stressed you were. It was like you were holding your breath, waiting for the moment when you could let in the air again.

When you told me, I didn't feel sad in the beginning. I felt a great responsibility to hold your secret, entrusted with something valuable that I was determined to honour.

I don't remember how, when and where we said goodbye. When I walked into your apartment a day or two after you left, it still smelled like you guys. It was like you were there but you weren't, like your spirits and the memories of you in that place still lingered. Some of your things were there too. In the kitchen and in the living room. Traces of you for me to say goodbye to.

It was at this moment that I felt the separation. I cried and cried for what this place had meant for me.

Your Dafna apartment was a place of safety and love and creativity where I was truly inspired by you and what you do and who you are. A place where I could question things out loud. A place where I could be curious about the big world you knew so much about and tell you about the little world you found confusing and sinister.

When I was with you, things felt possible. You said I translated a world and a culture you couldn't understand. You too, my dearest Shell, you translated a world I could only imagine. You made the thoughts and dreams I had about a different life seem plausible and legitimate. You gave them words. The words that killed your friend Sam and made you leave South Africa were the words that made me feel alive when I was with you. They were the reason I had hope that one day I'd have my own words and that they'd mean something.

You and Paul had this amazing real-world experience that was tough and dangerous and yet you were still so tender and capable of so much kindness. I was always in awe of that and wondered how it was possible. Whenever I left your apartment after spending a few precious hours with you, Paul and little Tim, I felt lighter, unburdened by expectations, traditions and how I needed to armour up in a world that was hell-bent on moulding me into a certain shape. I felt a connection with you and something out there that I had no notion of. I felt heard and seen.

When I left your apartment that day for the last time, I felt empty. It was like stepping into the TARDIS, but it didn't take me anywhere. I got in my car and realised what I had lost: the space where I could be myself and where I could dream of bigger things. Where I could imagine myself beyond my limitations. It was the first time a loss has hit me that hard – it was a loss of your friendship and a loss of myself in that friendship.

Did I take the bookshelves you made out of two planks of wood and some cement bricks? Or did I just steal the idea from you? I can't remember. I took some books and the computer. I took your smiles and laughter and lightness and saved them up in my mind. 'There are people in the world who care about what you think and who you are – not just what you look like and how much you weigh and how religious you can be!' I told myself. 'There are people in the world who believe in you. Who think you can do more and be more. They're not here now, but they're out there in the world.'

When would *I* be out in the world? When would I break free and live a life that I wanted and where I made my own decisions? I tried to suppress these questions, but they kept coming up. As much as I wanted to believe something else was out there, I knew that the way I was meant to lead my life was prescribed by powers and people much stronger than me.

I was a young, single, Egyptian, Muslim woman … what chance did I have of living life my way when I was told beyond reasonable doubt that the minute I stepped out of my family's home was the minute I stepped into my husband's home – when I stopped being my family's responsibility, I'd start being the responsibility of a man.

That was my only way out. Even if I were to rebel, to branch out in my own against my family's wishes, which other women I know have done, some of them close friends, where would I have gone with a Third World passport? More and more women were doing even though it was frowned upon – but it was something I knew would destroy my mother – and what need did the world have for me anyway?

'Get married and study if you want,' my mother said when I told her that I wanted to do my masters abroad. 'Young women don't travel alone.'

'Why not? I asked. 'Says who?'

'Says religion, Shaimaa.' That was the end of that discussion. My sadness turned into anger. I felt trapped. Again. I realised that part of what I loved about being with you is that for a few hours I could feel un-trapped. I could feel like I had options.

In a way English has been my First World passport before I ever dreamed of getting my hands on one. English was the language of my imagination; it was my silent rebellion against my Arabic-speaking country and my Arabic-speaking region. It was part of the brochure of the Promised Land that is the West. With it, I could lose myself in Jane Austen novels, I could marvel at how Arundhati Roy sculpted the language like clay (how she knew all those words!).

I could pretend that because I loved the wit and feistiness of Meg Ryan in *You've Got Mail* and laughed at endless episodes of *Friends*, that maybe one day I could be that preppy and cute and unburdened.

English had the lightness of a freedom and possibilities that I was longing for and Arabic had the heaviness of a culture and society that, as beautiful and poetic as it is, I felt was shackling me. I've always felt jealous of my husband because he spoke and wrote beautiful Arabic. It came to him easily. It flowed so naturally. He also does calligraphy as a hobby! He always laughs at my childish handwriting when I write in Arabic. As I grew older my appreciation for Arabic and its intricacies grew. I realised after extensive use of the English language why I found Arabic so challenging. It was my mother tongue. The language by which I communicated with my family and friends, how we made jokes. But my thoughts were in English and so is my work. But like any bilingual person it allows you to occupy both worlds.

Arabic is one of the most difficult, richest and most beautiful languages in the world. It's an absolute privilege to be able to speak, read and write Arabic. My classical Arabic is atrocious I've been told. But my colloquial works just fine.

It's ironic that speaking English has helped my career in the Arabic-speaking world while Arabic has helped it in the English-speaking world. I still regret not having learned French. It remains the arrogant, beautiful, cool person who just doesn't want to be my friend.

I may wear English like my skin as you describe. I think of it more as a cape, or wings that I hoped would take me to a different place in reality like it has in my imagination. But English also eludes me often – every now and then I'm reminded that despite swimming in it, I am a foreign fish.

I may speak the language, but I am a foreigner to its history, to the twists of meanings and turns of phrase that only those born into it would have. It comes to me more naturally than Arabic sometimes – when Ahmed and I fight, for example, his jabs are in Arabic and I respond in English – and I guess we both win!

I don't feel I've mastered either language, though. I feel it when I lose words in the middle of a sentence or when I mix my metaphors or when English makes its way so incongruously into an Arabic conversation. When I was younger, I thought it was cool. A sign that I was bilingual and worldly. Now I know it's a sign of poor vocabulary.

I guess that's what happens when the permanent space you occupy is 'between' – between cultures, languages, countries, identities. You asked me before if I'm trying to write myself into wholeness. The honest answer is that I don't know if I can. There are so many fragments of myself and they belong in different places – some of them belong together and others don't.

A few days after I went to your empty apartment, I told myself I had to see you again. I didn't know how. I needed a plan …

# 34.

# SHELLEY

I know what happens when you go into a place recently vacated by people you love. There's always a ghostly after-image, an impression that is left behind — people who leave create a vacuum, and it can be hard to walk into that. It's like the wake turbulence of a jet — tossing those who follow around, turning them upside down.

We arrived in Pendleton, Oregon, USA. High desert. Dust. Few trees. Twelve inches of precipitation a year and mostly in the form of snow. As anticipated, many churches and a woollen mill. The Umatilla Indian Reservation. Cowboys with big pickups and gun racks cruising through town. An annual rodeo which was about to happen, and literally, the cowboys and Indians were gathering in town.

We eventually had to come in on a tourist visa. Paul would have to go back to London to get his H1 visa when that came through, because it was taking too long and classes were beginning and he was desperate not to lose this opportunity. Meanwhile, he couldn't get paid because he couldn't legally work. I can't believe the risks we took.

We stayed for the first week at Paul's colleague Caroline's bunkhouse, just outside of town. She had a horse and two dogs, and a sweet old cat called Ralph.

She was kind and compassionate from the moment we met and this made me want to cry.

The bunkhouse was a cabin. Comfortable with everything we needed. Outside there were chickens, tomato plants, and a view over the distant Blue Mountains.

On Caroline's kitchen table lay a pile of her mail.

Caroline Le Guin.

'Are you,' I asked her two days after we arrived, 'by any chance related to the author Ursula Le Guin?'

She looked at me and burst out laughing. 'Yes,' she said. 'She's my mother.'

'Your mother?'

The bunkhouse we were staying in.

I thought about my childhood in South Africa. I read every single book in the school library. I climbed the tree behind our house, looking over the rusty yellow winter grass and in that tree I sat and I read Ursula Le Guin's *Earthsea* trilogy, and imagined the world created by a writer thousands of miles across the oceans and continents. I never would have guessed it was the same writer whose weekend bunkhouse I would one day stay in.

I couldn't believe that Caroline, the kindest and humblest and most generous of people, was the daughter of the writer whose words I had devoured and cherished as a ten-year-old in South Africa.

It would be some months until I met Ursula.

And then later, Caroline and I would be invited to join a writing group with her. We became the Poultry Group – six fiction-writing chicks meeting once a month, who turned their hands to poetry. And in this group I would learn everything

I eventually came to know about writing craft. These fierce women taught me about the silences, the spaces between, the power of what lay behind written words, and how words that worked well disappear because they serve the purpose of transporting the reader into another realm.

So coming to America, in that sense, was an absolute gift, an unanticipated treasure. I was given a space in which to be a writing self, with five other women representing four decades, with their wisdom, their fierce unapologetic view of the world. In the group were feminists, a lesbian, all atheists and each divine – despite labels these writing women were to me feminine, sacred, unbound, spiritual in essence whether they believed it or not. I found a tribe to belong to in that group – a group where the only thing that bound us was our wordsmithing.

But of course, day-to-day living in Pendleton, Oregon was a different matter. We eventually rented a house from a cowboy.

When we signed the agreement, he called me Mrs Williams.

'I'm Davidow,' I said. 'Ms.'

'Well, you'll have to sign separate agreements then, if y'all aren't married.'

'We are married,' I said. 'I just kept my name. I'm a writer.'

'Well,' he said with a twang, 'you're an independent li'l lady.'

I wanted to grab the pen out of his hand and poke it in his eye.

Instead, I took it from him and quietly signed my name.

Paul taught at Blue Mountain Community College – English and Philosophy. I stayed at home and looked after Tim. I took him to the Children's Museum, and we ate at the Cookie Tree. I joined a group of mothers who took their kids to Kindermusik, but Tim didn't like the rough kids and I didn't like the parochial mums, so we pulled back on that. Early in the mornings sometimes, I took Tim to an old train yard and we walked through the rubble so he could collect nuts and bolts and rusted screws and so he could look at the couplings of an old caboose and check out how the wheels of the old train connected with the track and I thought, there's no social conditioning here – my child loves mechanics and at two, is interested in how the world works, whereas I am only concerned with whether the world works.

Paul was a one-hundred-per-cent father. The kindest. The most committed to Tim's wellbeing. He was kind to me too, but the hope of us finding each other and growing love again in the high desert of Oregon I put on hold – we were in survival mode, waiting first to get our visas, then to apply for Green Cards after paying thousands of dollars to an immigration attorney.

In my Poultry Group, assigned a different poetic form to write in each month, I started to write about the hemispheres I'd lived in. I found it healing to use these poetic limitations of form and structure to make my life into art.

Qatar was part of my dreams almost every night. The women and their stories haunted me.

### Qatari Women

Are they silhouettes
or black holes,
these stark tent shapes
against the dusty purple sky?

They drift apologetically
between fluorescent waves
and an upside-down Arabian moon.

And when a man approaches,
several figures huddle,

become a single, dark creature
as present and invisible
as the humid canopy of night.

The cluster breaks,
the man walks on
and several female forms
turn to watch
from the other side of an
abyss.

The purple horizon turns black —
becomes the void
into which they vanish.

As a young mother without residence, without any security at all, the poems became my escape. I thought of Ghalia and her forbidden poems. I had the luxury and privilege of being able to write poetry about anything and everything at any time.

We watched the turn of the century through the flames of a bonfire on Caroline's property. Paul played the guitar with frozen fingers and the snow clouds built. The horse, listening to the music, galloped around the paddock. I think she was happy. The year was 2000. Two decades back in time. I was learning that the Big Bad Patriarch still held me down under his thumb. There were expectations of what a young mother should be and do, who she should play with — she should of course go to Pampered Chef and Tupperware parties, and join a church. She should not be Jewish in a cowboy town. She should be a grown up and paint her nails. She should have another baby otherwise the first one will end up spoiled like he already is and demanding too much attention. She should not be concerned about politics or the nearby Umatilla Chemical

Weapons Depot, containing the seventh-largest stockpile in the world of nerve and sarin gas, designed to kill other people and their children, but now leaching into the ground and air and (don't say it) creating cancer clusters, and clusters of people with strange neurological disorders. She also should not be concerned with the nearby Hanford Nuclear Site – the largest of its kind in the world, and the underground radioactive plume moving unstoppably towards the Columbia River, already potentially one of the most radioactive waterways in the world, but no one wants to hear this. She should not listen to the youngsters who went fishing and kept catching two-headed trout and discovered mutations of fish as a result of radioactive waste. No, this was not supposed to bother her. And if the USA was contemplating starting some kind of a war sometime, probably in Iraq (because America had unfinished business there with Saddam Hussein so, my friends said, watch for some kind of warmongering if baby George Bush gets into power) the young mother was not supposed to be in the least bit concerned about these things.

So, America had unexpected treasures: my beloved writers, poetry.

It was also devastating.

*

I missed you then. I wanted to see you, talk to you. My isolation continued in new ways. We were sporadically in contact and I wanted you to come and visit, but I had little hope of that, dear Shaimaa. How would that ever have been possible, I thought. You were twenty, going on twenty-one, in Qatar, and I was a just-legal, non-working, non-citizen of the high desert of Eastern Oregon.

## Chemicals

### 1.

**Sheraton Beach Club, Doha, Qatar**

At the Sheraton Beach Club, you float out into the bay
Carried by warm, soupy Gulf waters –
Watch giant jellyfish drift –
Imagine blue sky far out somewhere beyond the yellow haze –
Imagine fish in these Gulf waters
Gazing perplexed at the casing of a stray missile
Buried under water
In sand
Saddam always shot wide of his mark.
He didn't get Kuwait.
But after the misplaced missiles
Entire species of fish
Died.
Swimmers developed strange diseases.
Some also
Died.

### 2.

**Umatilla Chemical Weapons Depot, Oregon**

These hunching turtle-shaped mounds along the freeway
Guard unhatched poison eggs
From whence dormant toxins escape
Decaying casings
Into groundwater –
And poisonous winds scatter slow, invisible death.
These turtle mounds: the progeny of men and women
Who dreamed up death for other people's children – faraway
children
Not their own living here, living near.

233

# 35.

# SHAIMAA

Back in 2001 it wasn't a lethal virus sweeping the world. It was terrorism. Al Qaeda was about to take centre stage and I was obliviously making my way to where it was going to happen.

My trip to DC. My gift to myself. My little big escape.

I'm smiling at the fact that, at one point, I thought my biggest hurdle was getting myself from Doha to the US.

I don't know which was the bigger challenge at the time: convincing my mother to let me travel to America on my own or convincing the US embassy in Doha to give me, a young, single Muslim woman, a visa to get in.

After you left Doha the void was almost unbearable. You, my TARDIS, my access to the real world had left the Doha bubble for the real world. I had missed you so so much and wanted to see you.

*

It was the summer of 2001 – when Doha and the Gulf are generally deserted as the holidays start. It's hard to tell if it's the

234

heat and humidity or the emptiness that crush your soul. Maybe both. Everything loses colour, the way an overcooked meal loses taste …

I'd just graduated and needed to do something. I was already working at the radio station. But I needed something else. Something profound. I needed to get out of the overheated bubble and see and do something different.

I wanted to travel alone. I wanted to experience something for myself. I wanted a story of my own. I wondered what it would be like to see you in the US. All the places we'd go. And the fun we'd have. It became my mission to visit you!

I was about to turn twenty-two. People my age travelled, met friends, met other people, spent days and nights away from the gaze and supervision of parents and it was normal.

But first I needed a plan. I called the embassy to ask if I was eligible for a visit visa and the man on the phone said, 'You're a young woman with no full-time job in Doha, no steady income and no real reason to come back. To be honest your chances are slim.'

*

So, my first mission was to find a summer job and to convince them to write me a reference letter, then convince the people at the embassy that I had enough ties to Qatar for me to come back …

I had to convince my mother to allow me to come and visit you, but first I needed to ask you. Without any hesitation you said I was welcome anytime. I had no idea how much you were struggling at the time. That this place I was trying to get to was a place that was already killing you inside.

*

I said to my mother that you had invited me to come and stay with you and celebrate my twenty-second birthday. I said to her I'd love to go, but understand how expensive it would be (I'm financially aware and responsible) but maybe if I save enough money and take another job (hard work and frugality; equally strong anchors for the story) we could think about it? We'll see …

I can't remember how my mother reacted at first – but I must've been convincing enough throughout the summer because when I told her I had enough money to buy the ticket she said it was okay and asked what I would do about the visa.

So there I was. Last week of August. Embassy appointment made.

Papers in order: bank statement, reference letter, address in the US, ticket and my story of a visit to my former teacher which was my birthday gift to myself after graduating with an English degree from Qatar University and before coming back to my job as an ESL teacher.

I was so nervous on my way to the fortress that is the embassy. I'd driven by its high external walls before but never thought to go through the gates ever.

'You can't look desperate,' I told myself. 'Act casual. Bored even. Like you didn't care if this happened or not, like you didn't spend your whole summer planning it. Like this was an afterthought …'

An Egyptian couple with their baby daughter sat in the row just ahead of me.

Then it was my turn at the window.

'Hi,' I said with the most casual American air I could muster.

'Hi. Where's the accent from?' The woman asked. I was in.

'Miami, I guess. I spent some time there when my mum was a PhD student,' I said.

'Is that so?' She smiled. A good sign, I thought. 'So you want to visit the US,' she said, looking at my papers.

'Yeah,' I said, looking at the papers too, trying really hard to steady my voice.

'I'm visiting my old teacher. It's my birthday gift to me!'

'Oh, happy birthday. So, you don't plan on seeking work in America?'

'No.' I said with a look that said, *Oh, don't be absurd.*

'Do you plan on studying in America?' she asked.

'Ah, no thanks. I just graduated. I've done enough studying for a while … ha ha.' A joke, I thought, could help. Maybe.

My story was going well.

'So, tell me about your job,' she said.

'Yeah, so I started this summer and my manager is so kind he's giving me a few weeks off. Teaching English as a second language is really interesting because you get to deal with different ages and nationalities. I get to be all bossy … ha ha!' Another joke landed.

'Nice. Well good luck with it all. Come and pick up your passport and visa in four days.'

'Oh. Cool, thanks. Bye,' I said.

I was breathing so heavily on my way to the car. It was the heat and the nerves. Did I just pull this off? Could I pull the rest of it off too?

# 36.

# SHELLEY

Our lives in Pendleton, Oregon lay physically and metaphorically in the rain shadow. All the moisture fell on the western side of the Cascade mountain range. No water made it over the peaks of the mountains that rose 10,000 feet into the air, or hardly any.

In this high desert amid wheat fields and waving grass, I learned things I didn't want to know. Things you would not easily find on the internet in those days, about what it meant to live in relative proximity to the Hanford Nuclear Site and the Umatilla Chemical Weapons Depot.

A blowing dust area thirty miles away from our home on Northwest Twenty-First Street and along the interstate had signs that warned people to keep their car windows closed. Radioactive dust was a hazard that closed windows might, perhaps, protect against.

Recent studies reveal that plutonium, thorium and uranium are showing up in the dust in households and on hiking trails near the waste facilities – impacting 'down-winders', those who live down wind of such facilities. These particles sift into lungs and bodies and can cause radioactive damage to the tissues where they lodge, undetectable by scanners.

Soon after we first saw the signs, they were taken down. Apparently, people were upset. By the signs.

No one wanted to talk about the leaking chemical weapons. The Umatilla Chemical Weapons Depot lay thirty miles to the west of us, the seventh-largest stockpile in the nation. Driving to and from Portland for weekend trips, we passed acres of weapons buried in ominous mounds. Corroding warheads with nerve gas, sarin gas that would never be used. I couldn't imagine designing and making these. Who goes to work fantasising about the best way to damage mothers and fathers and children in distant countries? Now those weapons lay, sleeping monsters leaching their poisons into the ground and air – toxins making their insidious way into the bodies of the very Americans they were supposedly designed to protect.

The weapons would be incinerated before long. Hence the emergency billboard signs on I-84 and the sirens to warn of a disaster, if one occurred. Testing was being carried out.

A year after we left Oregon, a year after I was sick, in September 2004, the army began incinerating nearly 4000 tons of chemical agent. They completed the destruction of the chemical munitions finally in October 2011, and I wasn't there to see it.

Perhaps while we were living there, the green mustard haze that hung in the air had nothing to do with weapons or nuclear waste.

I learned not to talk about Hanford or the depot. Or the new cancer centre that was being planned as part of a massive expansion to the St Mary Medical Centre in Walla Walla, forty-five minutes from Pendleton. The patient load of cancer victims in the area was significant. Cancer cells don't come with tags attached to them, linking this cancer to Hanford, or that one to Umatilla. Making such connections would be conjecture.

The First World. Finally. A safe place I had been wanting to reach since I vowed to leave Africa.

I was on an H2 visa: the wife of someone allowed to work, but not allowed to work myself – a temporary resident without rights, floating and hovering, unable to put down roots. I hid under my jeans and T-shirts, the heavy burden I felt of having No Where to Go.

I think I did a pretty good job at playing the role of young stay-at-home mother. As if I had a choice. As if I wasn't full of fear that we would not be able to renew our visa, afford the thousands of dollars required for a Green Card, an application that did not in any way guarantee success. As if I was exactly the same as any middle-class, stay-at-home young mother.

Our picturesque A-frame house stood on a hill next to Pendleton High School and across a small valley from the community college where Paul taught.

Summers were as hot and dry as Qatar's were hot and humid.

The distant Blue Mountains and hills were as tawny as lion fur. Sometimes they reminded me of the Highveld in South Africa.

There were kind people and they made us feel welcome.

But I was living again caught between the proverbial frying pan and the fire – between that old rock and hard place. You wanted this, I told myself. You wanted to get into the First World. You have arrived in the First World. Welcome, Third World Child.

Dare I admit that I missed the connections that were forged in Doha? I missed you, dear Shaimaa, coming over to drink tea and sit on our light-green carpeted apartment floor while Tim crawled into your lap. I missed my students.

I didn't understand what a dichotomy I was. In my Eastern Oregon rain shadow life, I passed easily for one of the locals on any given day. As long as I didn't open my mouth.

'You have such a cool accent,' people said. 'Where are you from?'

Every day.

I tried to see the value in the half-friendships I formed with the young mothers who echoed media propaganda: Pendleton is a great place to raise kids. It's so safe, so nice. Aside from nearby nuclear waste and leaking chemical weapons.

That which was invisible could never be held responsible for harming you.

### 7 September, 2001

In the dream, I'm on a plane. I stand in a centre aisle, looking towards the cockpit, my hands resting on the tops of the seats on either side of me. In front of my face, without warning, a swirling fireball – red, yellow, green. I can't move. I am immobilised in the middle of the plane's fuselage while everything disintegrates around me.

We woke on a rainy day in Norfolk. 8 September, 2001. We were in England on a visit to Paul's elderly parents. We had travel documents to allow us out of America while we were in the process of applying for Green Cards.

In the upstairs room of their small flat, looking out over a green meadow where a white horse grazed on grass and daisies, I folded our clothes and packed them into a suitcase. I was thinking of you.

Finally, after two years of not seeing you, you were coming to visit. I couldn't quite believe that you would be coming from Doha, Qatar, to a small town in Oregon, to stay with us for your hard-earned holiday. The thought of seeing you in a few days wasn't enough to banish the knot in my stomach.

'I'm scared of flying back,' I said to Paul. 'I had a nightmare last night. About a fireball rushing at me inside a plane.'

Paul looked at me. 'What does that mean?'

'I don't know. I'm anxious.'

'Do you think we shouldn't fly?'

'I think we can fly. But I'm afraid something terrible is about to happen – with a plane. Somewhere.'

At Heathrow, we waited in long lines. I watched two Gulf Arab men in their white dishdashas swan past me straight into the women's toilets. Then they came out laughing. They were wandering around, these young men, exuding restless energy – impervious to rules and regulations and societal expectations. They walked past us talking so loudly we couldn't have our own conversation.

'I hope these guys aren't on our flight,' I said to Paul when we were called to board. 'They seem out of control and they smell of smoke.'

They were on our flight all the way from London to Vancouver, BC.

Then they were on a small flight to Portland, Oregon.

As we took off, one of the guys went to the female flight attendant and asked her something. I overheard her say: 'Once we reach cruising altitude, you're welcome to visit the cockpit.'

I looked at Paul. 'That feels completely unsafe,' I said. 'How can they allow this?'

We reached cruising altitude, and the one man went right into the cockpit with an air of entitlement and sat in the jump seat.

'I don't like this,' I said.

'Maybe he's a pilot,' Paul said.

'Isn't this weird?'

'It's very strange.'

I said, 'He could just knock out the pilots and take control of the plane. I hate this.'

'Relax,' said Paul. 'I'm sure we'll be fine.'

At passport control, an official asked the two men to step aside.

Then our turn, exhausted and jet lagged with a tired four-year-old and I hoped for a speedy way through customs.

'Can you come this way please?'

'Pardon?'

'Please come with us.'

'Us?'

'Who do you think I'm talking to?' The US Immigration official escorted us to a small room.

We waited there with the men from the flight for two hours.

They were questioned first.

Then us.

They left their interrogation before we did.

Hours of high-stress waiting and questioning with an exhausted child after a long international journey, and then another hour later, we finally left the airport for a three-hour drive back to Pendleton.

'I don't want to fly again. I hate having a Third World passport,' I said when we arrived home. 'If I didn't have a South African passport, we would have been treated with more respect.' We carried a sleeping Tim to his room.

*

On 9 September 2001, you called me and gave me your flight details.

Arriving 11 September in Portland, Oregon. We would drive the three hours back to Portland to pick you up. I was so looking forward to having you stay.

On the morning of September 11, I woke up.

Paul was in the basement watching TV.

As I entered the room, he switched it off.

'What?'

'Nothing.'

'No, come on, what?'

'Your dream … there was a plane crash. But apparently an accident. A small plane crashed into one of the Twin Towers in New York.'

'Please can you turn on the TV again, I want to see.'

Reluctantly, Paul obliged.

'Oh,' he said. 'It wasn't a small plane.'

While we were watching, the second plane hit the second tower.

Another hour later, you called. 'I'm in Washington DC,' you said, tearful, anxious. 'I can see smoke from the Pentagon.'

# 37.

# SHAIMAA

The trip to DC was long and exhausting. We transited in Amsterdam and I remember being really nervous about being at the wrong gate and missing my plane. It was my first time ever in a European airport.

I loved all the Dutch trinket airport shops. Of course, I bought the mandatory fridge magnets: windmill, clogs and red-light district – the honey waffles in the red and blue tin can which I finished on the second leg of the trip. I was both fascinated and intimidated by the buzz of Schiphol airport. I was lost in all the anticipation, dread and excitement.

I was going to make a stop in Washington, DC for a couple of days, see the sights and then come and spend time with you and celebrate my birthday.

What I didn't know was that probably around the same time I was getting ready to start my American adventure, nineteen hijackers were getting ready to board four planes to launch coordinated attacks on the US – setting in motion a chain of events that would wreak havoc in America and carnage in the Middle East and Afghanistan for years to come.

The countdown had already started. History and my little trip to freedom were about to take a disastrous turn.

*

I remember being on the phone to you on my third day. I had plans to go see the Washington Monument or the Lincoln Memorial. Maybe I'd walk by Pennsylvania Ave and see the White House.

I was slowly beginning to realise how out of my depth I was. I was an inexperienced traveller. All alone.

*

The morning of September 11, I was half awake when I saw what looked like a huge chimney with thick smoke billowing on TV.

I changed the channel. Same footage. I sat up and realised that this was a building apparently on fire – the presenter saying something about 'unconfirmed reports that a plane crashed into the World Trade Center in New York'.

Every channel had now turned to the breaking news. No one seemed to know what was going on and I was in bed trying to think of a place to have breakfast before setting out to visit some sights.

More news coming in. Eyewitnesses and news reporters on the phone, sounding flustered, describing what they'd seen and heard. A loud bang. Glass and windows shattering and huge plumes of smoke.

One woman was describing what she saw. She said, 'Oh my God. Another plane just hit the other building. Right in the middle of it. Explosion. My God. Right in the middle of it.'

The female anchor gasped.

A second plane. This time it was caught on live television. It hit the south tower at the World Trade Centre. People screaming. New Yorkers on the streets looking up, watching in horror as their city was attacked in a way very few could have imagined.

I sat on the bed, eyes fixed on the TV, unsure what was happening. Unsure what to do. I don't know how much time passed as I sat there. But then I started hearing sirens; they felt so close. I went to the window seat where I'd spent most of the last four days.

In the distance I saw what looked like smoke and I didn't understand. Was there a fire here too? An explosion? Wasn't this just in New York? This attack? Was something happening here too? What do I do? Where do I go?

I went back to the TV. The Pentagon was hit. Another plane. This time hitting America's mighty Department of Defence. A blatant slap in the face of the world's strongest military power.

News reporter: 'There's a lot of confusion here at the Pentagon. It appears that something hit on the outside of the fifth corridor, the army corridor. The Pentagon has been evacuated. Several people are trapped.'

Another news reporter: 'We also have a report now that it was a plane that crashed into the Pentagon. We have a large fire at the Pentagon.'

Channels were now rotating footage – scenes at the Pentagon, then New York City, where the Twin Towers were on fire. Eyewitnesses described blasts, one saying she saw people jump out of the windows to save themselves.

A few more minutes or hours. I had no idea. The sound of sirens outside my window still so loud. Smoke.

The first tower collapsed. A huge mushroom of smoke and debris ... Anchors and reporters struggling for words ... Me struggling to get up and go to the window.

Then the second one. The whole thing felt unreal. If this was a scene in an action film, it would've been a bit over the top.

But it wasn't a film. Someone took a knife and landed it at the heart of New York and the whole world was watching in real time.

'Good lord,' the CNN anchor said as the towers peeled away into thick explosive powder. 'There are no words.'

Of all the things I've heard and seen on the day and the years that followed, this scene and those words stuck with me. Sometimes there are no words.

I couldn't speak. I had no one to speak to anyway.

I just sat there. Dazed.

What do I do? Leave. To where? Go to Shelley? But flights were being cancelled. Would I be able to get onto a plane at all after what happened?

Good Lord. There are no words.

Chaos, in my head and on the screen. The Twin Towers were sinking like my heart. My mother! That's what I needed to do. Call my mother. Tell her I was okay.

Mum heard the news and hadn't heard from me. I turned my phone off so as not be charged internationally (no airplane mode at the time) so she called you.

How do I reassure her that nothing happened? I finally gathered enough courage to call home.

*

I can't remember a word she said. All I remember was her voice. She'd clearly been crying – worried sick. But she was pulling herself together, her words were shaky but resolved. God, how strong my mother is.

'I'm okay, Mummy,' was all I could muster.

'If you can come home now, do, habibty,' she said.

'Sure … I'll try, Mummy, but it's okay. I still can go to Shelley too. She says it's fine.'

'Okay. See what you can do.'

As my taxi pulled over near the domestic terminal, queues were snaking all around the parking lot. People had been camping out from the night before. I was there at around 4 am and got to the check-in desk around 10.

One of the very few things I do remember is a conversation between two women in the airport queue which had the words *Al Qaeda, Bin Laden, Arabs, the Middle East* and how 'it'll be hell' or something to that effect.

I looked at the women and said, 'But I am from the Middle East'.

'Well! I got bad news for you honey … it's gonna get real nasty,' one of the women said, in the understatement of the century.

*

The trip from DC to Oregon would've taken about five-and-a-half hours with one or two stops. I think my original flight had one stop in Seattle. When I finally arrived at the check-in desk and showed my ticket, the woman said that this was all cancelled now.

I looked at her in horror and said that I needed to get to Oregon please and was there any way I could be put on another flight please even if there were multiple transits.

'Please. I'll take anything.'

'Okay! I'm just doing that now for you ma'am.' She pointed sharply at the screen and ogled me in a look that said, *I'm doing the best I can — just calm the fuck down.*

I know she sensed my despair but it was clear she was reaching the end of her tether too.

*

Everything after that was a complete blur; I honestly don't know how many flights I took from the East to the West Coast. I know that there were so many that I no longer worried about transits – I either just followed the crowd or asked my way through all the airports. In the moments I was awake on any given plane I'd know we were in a different state because of the weather changes. There was rain, then sun, then overcast skies, then darkness ... Or maybe that was me passing out from stress and fatigue. I was becoming a more experienced traveller in the worst possible manner.

*

I followed the crowd again in Portland airport. Then I don't know why I decided to turn around to ask the officer something.

An alarm immediately went off. 'Stop! You can't go back that way ma'am,' the officer yelled.

And then you and Paul appeared as if magically.

'Oh, what kind of trouble are you trying to get into now?' you said with open arms and that beautiful smile of yours.

I just ran to you ... I ran and hugged you so tight. In the middle of this upheaval, this was exactly where I needed to be.

# 38.

# SHELLEY

When you finally came to America I was like a person without a lifejacket in messy, wild seas, wanting to take you with me to the safe shoreline, barely able to stay afloat myself.

So, while you were in Oregon, while America reeled in the aftermath of 9/11, we used our time together as a sanctuary. We talked, ate, laughed and shared Doha memories.

You'd finished your degree. Now you'd caught up with me. Both of us wanted to do a masters. I wished I was a millionaire. I would have bought us the opportunities to do post-grad degrees at top universities and we could have studied at the same time.

Our cat Mimi terrorised you at night scratching on your door. I'm so sorry! A trip to America would not be complete for you, I thought, without doing something daring, something that we could never have done in Qatar. So, I did the most outrageous thing I could think of: I drove you out to the Umatilla Reservation where there was a casino, a garish structure in the midst of tawny wheat fields. You were wearing a sleeveless shirt. We entered the noisy, plush-carpeted room. While the world reeled outside, you and I mischievously slipped quarters into a slot-machine. It wasn't long before a security guard approached us. 'Ma'am,' he said to me. 'Can I see some ID?'

You laughed. I looked at him and pointed at my face, annoyed. 'Does this look like under twenty-one to you? Does it?'

'Well, I don't see many wrinkles.'

We lost our money happily for the next couple of hours.

A few days later, continuing our quest for daring activities, we went into a bar on Main Street. Cowboys, the bartender and a moose head on the wall watched us accusingly as we made our way to the pool table. The bartender approached us. She asked you for your ID.

'I don't have one on me,' you said. We had decided that having no ID was better than showing a Middle Eastern passport or ID document at this point in time.

'She's old,' I said. 'She just has a baby face.' We laughed, but it didn't get us anywhere and we were kicked out of the bar.

We took you to the markets in Portland and we bought tie-dye shirts.

We browsed through different shades of the American dream in the shadow of 9/11. Being with you meant that the rest of the world and its drama played out as background noise while we ate sushi and caught trams through Portland and then drove the three hours back to Pendleton along the Columbia River.

I had no idea that it would be a decade before we'd see each other again.

Your leaving was as dramatic as your arrival, reflecting the fact that I didn't want to let you go.

The night I dropped you off at the Greyhound station to go back to Qatar, via Portland and Washington, Main Street in Pendleton was empty, except for us. It was near midnight. Suddenly, behind us, flashing lights, red, white and blue – and sirens. A cop car. Shit. I pulled over.

I rolled down the window to the stony-faced police officer.

'Ma'am could you get out of the car please?'

You stared out from the shadows, your big, brown eyes watching. I felt you go small, invisible. It's a talent – vanishing in plain sight – a habit learned, perhaps, from knowing how not to draw attention, how to pull all your energy inward, until you're almost cloaked in invisibility. I had never known someone to do that before.

'Why, what have I done?' My heart raced. My mouth was dry.

'What have you done? Are you serious?'

'Yes.'

He looked skyward as if asking for help. 'You don't know what you've done?'

'No.'

'Ma'am. Get out of the car, please. You drove all the way down Main Street on the left-hand side of the road.'

I hadn't noticed. In shock, I had to admit that, indeed, there I was. Parked facing the wrong way on the wrong side of the road. How had this happened? There was no traffic to follow. I was talking to you, my dear Shaimaa – I must have been feeling at home, and when feeling at home, maybe I thought that made me drive on the left as I did when I was young.

'Oh.'

'I want you to walk along here in a straight line.'

My legs shook so much I could barely walk in a straight line.

'Follow my finger with your eyes.' I watched his finger make circles in front of my face. I was aware of you in the car. What if they pulled you out too? Where are you from? What's your name? What's a young Muslim girl from the Gulf doing in Pendleton a week after 9/11?

I passed the breathalyser test.

Shaking, dizzy with fear, and apologetic I spoke in soft English-accented tones.

'I am terribly sorry.'

'Ma'am, I could cite you for four moving violations,' the beefy officer said.

'I'm so sorry, again,' I said. 'We just got back from England and I'm still jet lagged and was having a moment of confusion. You're right to pull me over. I really should not be driving right now.' Of course, he thought I was English. To almost every single American I'd met I was English or Australian – though I'd never been to Australia. Once someone thought I was French – but no one so far had guessed at the reality: I was an escapee from the African continent. My accent was South African. My passport bound me to a land I was doing everything I could to break free from. But no one seemed to be able to tell.

He looked at me suddenly in a fatherly way. My accent hung in the air between us. He took out a book. Wrote something. Tore it off and handed it to me. No fines. Just a written note to warn me of what could have happened. I looked up.

'Thank you,' I said.

Was this it? Did we look innocuous enough? Two young women at midnight driving empty streets on the wrong side, one Muslim, one Jew, just after the attacks, both of us having been in Qatar, me without a permanent resident visa, married to someone on an H1 work visa who also recently worked in the Gulf, not even knowing which side of the road to drive on – this, in a conservative cowboy town? I don't know, but if I were a cop stalking these streets, I'd have thought the situation worthy of further investigation.

'Can we go?'

'Get outta here,' he said.

I tried not to cry. 'Thanks.'

'Welcome ma'am. You have a good night now. Get some sleep and in future, don't drive tired.'

Privilege is when you are not seen as 'other'. In this moment, I was acutely aware of not being seen as 'other'. This was because although I felt other, outside, no identity but one of an escapee, a non-resident with no rights, skin tone and words and accent perhaps acted as a shield. Would I have been wished a good night had I been black or dark brown with a different accent under these circumstances? I have my doubts.

I dropped you off at the bus station and hugged you goodbye. Was I crazy, letting you go out alone into the wild west to find your way back? But you were a tough, courageous young woman. Who was I to undermine your autonomy by my fears?

I missed you already. When would I ever see you again?

I drove home, shaken by the dissonance between my desperate geographically dislocated self and the calm English-speaking person who politely apologised to the cop and wasn't hit with fines for four moving violations.

*

We spent three years in Pendleton.

My poetry group in Portland was made up of award-winning novelists, poets and memoir writers. I went there once a month and these writer friends became my lifeline.

One of Paul's colleagues was diagnosed with a malignant brain tumour. She was a runner – a fit and healthy mother and writer. But over twelve months, I got to know her as someone almost blind, wandering around the room from chair to chair, trying to escape what she described as unbearable pain. Eventually she died. I read one of her poems out at her funeral.

This was supposed to be a safe place to live. Radioactive and chemical waste are not the same as a guy with a machete or a machine-gun (I say guy because it's rarely a woman who goes on the rampage), but I felt like I was in constant danger.

Then I got sick.

The pituitary tumour in my head did not arrive with tags attached to the extra cells that pointed directly to aforementioned environmental pollutants. But, like the colleague of Paul's who died, my first symptoms were visual disturbances that were as indescribable as a dream you can't quite remember.

Unlike the colleague's tumour, mine was benign.

It was threatening because of where it was – in close proximity to the optic nerve.

For five months I couldn't see properly out of my left eye. I stopped driving. I went into a dark place and I did not know if I would ever come out. After months of no sleep and treatments and trying to heal not just my body, but my soul, I began to recover.

But I knew I had to run away again. I knew I could not stay here if I was going to heal. I did not want to live anymore in this fallout/downwind zone where something you could neither see, feel nor taste could slowly erode your life.

In southern Africa, a sangoma – a medicine man – once told me that if you are ill, you need to go back to the earth where you were born, to reset yourself, your body – to get in touch with who you are and why you are on the planet.

I didn't want to go back to South Africa. But I wanted to go south, to be warm again. To look up at the arc of night and see stars I recognised.

And the love that was lost in the desert – it lay underneath, a deep river.

Paul took care of me and Tim with every part of himself while I struggled with my health. When I said I need to live in a warm place again, he applied for jobs all over.

I didn't want to lose my writer friends, but I had already lost so much.

I wanted my health back. I wanted to be a good mum – a living mum.

Once I had been diagnosed with a tumour, my health insurance dropped me. No one else would insure me because I had a pre-existing condition.

I began to feel that sense of desperation again. I wanted to run away.

My youngest brother, living in Australia, said to me on the phone, 'I reckon you guys would like it here.'

I called an immigration lawyer.

'Do you have any secretarial skills?'

'No,' I said.

'What do you do?'

'I'm a writer.'

'A writer? Are you published?'

'Around thirty books.'

'You might be eligible for a Distinguished Talent visa. I can't see you qualifying with enough points otherwise.'

I did not know what that was, but when I hung up, I researched this visa and decided that I would apply without the lawyer's help or fees. It looked straightforward.

# 39.

# SHAIMAA

Pendleton was a haze. I do, however, remember that I enjoyed playing with little Timmy on the deck where he pretended the chairs were rockets and spaceships ... I should've known that this boy was going to be a pilot one day. I also remember that your garden was an open field and that I found that greenery healing. I don't think I'd processed what happened. The sound of the sirens near the Pentagon and the smoke would flash up but I would quickly push them down and think about something else.

I convinced myself that this constant knot in my stomach while I was in Oregon, and the random shakes that would hit me in the middle of the day and my inability to sleep, were just me being tired because of all the travelling. Not traumatised. Tired. I was also very, very worried about my mother.

As the US and the world reeled from the aftermath of the 9/11 attacks, I realised that I'd turned twenty-two and that this age was forever going to be attached to one of the strangest and most traumatic experiences of my life particularly, I felt, because it was of my own doing.

The world was falling apart and here I was in this quiet town where hardly anything seemed to happen. I took walks with you. We spent a Saturday in an open market in Portland.

I watched you make a life for yourself with Paul and Tim in Pendleton. It was beautiful to see you move freely, unburdened by who might look at you or harass you. Although it struck me that you didn't enjoy it as much as I thought you would after Doha.

You and Paul were lovely and generous hosts. You tried very hard to take my mind off how dark this visit had turned. I tried to make the most of my time with you and remind myself that in the middle of the chaos unfolding in my head and in the White House Situation Room – as frontlines were being drawn and a new era of bloodshed loomed – it was actually sort of a miracle that I made it all the way to your house in Pendleton. I got to spend time with you and report back on the land you managed to escape and that I was somehow going to have to find my way back to. It was almost as if our friendship flourished under these extraordinary circumstances …

# 40.

# SHELLEY

My recovery from the tumour in my head and my plans to escape Pendleton were the same journey. Each step away from the chemical fallout zone was a step towards my freedom from illness and distress. We left Pendleton in the biggest snowstorm the Pacific Northwest had seen in decades. The man de-icing the plane fell off the stairs and the plane skidded to the left on the runway as it took off into zero visibility.

When I tried to look into the future – zero visibility.

# 41.

# SHAIMAA

When I flew back to Doha I was determined to move on. More importantly I wanted my mother and my sister to forget that this happened. I wanted to take away their anxiety and sleepless nights worrying about me in the US as Al Jazeera beamed those images of the collapsing Twin Towers and the wrath of America and the threats of war on loop. My sister told me – I can't remember when exactly – that she'd heard Mum praying and crying at night for my safe return. I still feel guilty – but how could I have known?

I wanted to prove to her that I was a good daughter. That I'd learned from this and would never do it again. I wanted to say all of that without saying it.

I was teaching English and continued to work at the radio station.

I started wearing the headscarf. It was around the time when the 'Modern Muslim Televangelists' dominated the airwaves. Cultural identity politics was at its height post 9/11 and I wanted to prove – as these men on TV preached – that you could be a good Muslim and a modern citizen of the world. And 'good Muslim' meant covering for women. 'A covered hip-hop radio DJ – that would be unusual!' I thought. My mother was delighted I started wearing the headscarf. On some level I felt I owed it to her.

I sat through what felt like endless family meetings for arranged marriage proposals both in Doha and back home in Alexandria. I was surprised how, after the first engagement fell apart, they were still determined to get me married that way. I learned how to smile and joke when my mother and aunties chastised me for saying no to yet another marriage offer.

During that time, I also met a fellow Egyptian who worked in the newsroom at Qatar Radio. Ahmed was adorable and knowledgeable, but I saw us more as friends. I never thought we'd be romantically involved. He was in his early twenties when we met and had the mannerisms of a forty-five-year-old history professor – a know-it-all with a *very* questionable fashion sense, which I would like to think I had a hand in changing throughout the years we've been married.

And yet he was the one I enjoyed talking to the most – he was annoyingly and so beautifully nerdy and bookish and had encyclopaedic knowledge about everything from Fellini films to the warplanes used in Operation Desert Storm. Mostly though, he was a nice guy – decent and kind and interested in me and all my crazy ideas.

I slowly realised that intellect and kindness were 'my thing' above all other things.

I fell in love with this beautiful, kind cinema geek. He was amused by my love of hip-hop even though he was not a fan himself. He took an article I wrote just for myself to the local English newspaper and got it published. He encouraged me to write. He listened. He did all the things that those who love you do without saying the words.

I resisted that love for a long time. Its ease and purity scared me, so I walked away. After years of back and forth and months without speaking to each other, I heard from a colleague that Ahmed was leaving for London. I called him and said I wanted to say goodbye and leave things on a positive note. He agreed and then asked if I wanted to go with him. So I did.

Of course, it wasn't as simple as that. Imagine if I just took off with him!

My mother was delighted when I told her the news that (finally!) someone wanted to marry me and I wanted to marry them. You could tell she was happy, not by her open expression of happiness, which of course she'd almost never show, but because of how curious she was. *Where did you meet him? What does his father do? Where is his mother? Oh, she's here? Oh, she wants to meet me? Okay then. Tell him to tell them it's okay to call and set up a time to meet.*

Then she called my uncle – as of course there needed to be a male family representative – who flew in from Saudi Arabia to be there for our small engagement the next week. My mother was admirably practical and efficient about the whole thing.

Ahmed then flew to London and after we signed a couple of papers long distance to show our families, the government and the world, we were married. I followed him a few months after. No wedding, much to the big family's disappointment. I was finally leaving Doha. But I realised I was also leaving my mother and sister and a piece of my heart behind.

# 42.

# SHELLEY

On the long flight to the opposite side of the world, I stared at the sky. I lost track of time, of days. Somewhere in the darkness, we crossed the equator. I looked out of the window and saw the Southern Cross. I saw Orion. The moon was the right way up. Familiar Southern Hemisphere constellations appeared once again in the blue-black sky.

We arrived in Sydney having left everything. Again. We had no jobs, no income. We had $17,000 in the bank. The story may as well have been a repeat of leaving South Africa. Or Qatar (except then we had a job we were going to). I don't know how we did this. I know that the fear of not doing it was greater than the fear of leaping off the edge into nothing.

Because nothing was not nothing.

Permanent residence in a country with a social welfare system that was not yet as greedy or corrupt or dysfunctional as the ones I'd left behind – that felt like everything to me. I had been granted residence on the basis of my writing. A Distinguished Talent visa was something I had not heard of and when I did, I imagined that it was designed for someone other than me.

Arriving on Australian soil as a writer, as someone valued for their words ... this too, was not nothing.

We landed in Sydney.

July. It was cold, in a familiar, South African way. The sea was a sharp and brilliant blue reflecting the naked sun in a billion glittering reflections. The city smelled of fumes and earth and saltwater.

The suburbs the taxi took us through made me depressed. Rows and rows of small brick houses hunched against the expansiveness of a Southern Hemisphere sky as though they couldn't bear the light, the space.

It was as though someone had taken a confined British suburb, stuck it on an African landscape and added a small taste of American sports car culture. It was familiar and disorienting – an ele-hippo-croca-duck stuck-together place where much of it seemed familiar, but where none of it seemed to belong together.

We were jet lagged. Tim had a migraine.

I felt lost.

A few days after we arrived, we drove to Byron Bay. We had rented a house on fifteen acres because I had seen the area from Google Earth, and judging by the expanse of beaches, hills and the proximity of two private schools I could apply to work in, we chose this place.

$17,000 between us and nothing. We feared running aground. But we were used to catching waves and being dumped.

*

Within the first few weeks of being in my new country I found a part-time teaching job in a leafy small school tucked into a tropical hillside near Byron Bay.

The children were wild. Teaching them meant re-inventing the idea of school.

Our rented house was deep in the bush. Mulberries, papayas and mandarins fell from the trees like gifts each morning.

One night, a three-metre-long python cruised over my head along a beam on the verandah, and I almost fainted with shock.

But also, with relief.

I was back. My African self had been dormant for so long that I had forgotten that once I, too, was wild. I had forgotten that I grew up with puff adders and boomslang and crocodiles and lions in the bush, and that I was not a stranger to big spiders and fat geckos that dropped onto your bed at night from the ceiling.

Australia, I learned, was the home of many living creatures that could kill you with their toxins – not least of which were redback and funnel-web spiders, and paralysis ticks, each of which could potentially kill or maim both small and large humans. There were other stings and hurts that came our way in our new land. Bullying was an issue both at school for Tim and at work for me. The third school Tim went to in that first year was a public school in the hinterland of Byron, where a super-strict principal with zero tolerance for bullying allowed him to flourish. He quickly outperformed all his peers in literacy, numeracy, music, drama. A group of wild boys with good hearts became his friends.

I eventually connected with a group of like-minded colleagues who were smart and funny and supportive. I also introduced creative writing to my teen students. Their literacy skills grew as did their realisation that each person had a unique, inimitable voice and a story to tell. They grew to love writing and I loved to teach it. There was something cathartic for me in the moments where I was aware of holding a space where, especially girls of thirteen, had the freedom to write whatever they wanted. One day one of my colleagues said to me, 'Bella read out her latest story to me. It's brilliant. It's really dark, though.'

'In what way is it dark, do you think?'

'Oh, it's all about depression – so evocative and passionate. I guess it's better out than in.'

'You have no idea,' I said.

Meanwhile, Paul still had not found work and we lived frugally, with barely enough income to cover rent and food, driving our old Toyota, bought for $3000, and praying it wouldn't break down. We walked on the beach. We breathed clean air.

I was grateful for many things – not least of which was Medicare. Rich and poor, regardless of colour, doctors and hospitals were available to anyone. No fancy insurance needed in an emergency. Compassion in doctor's offices. I learned I was living in a country where being poor or sick or vulnerable did not mean you could not get medical care. Affordable healthcare was not a luxury item in Australia, but a human right. No one asked for my insurance card at the doctor's office.

After eighteen months in the Byron Bay area, I was headhunted for a job in Queensland.

We drove to Noosa, on the Sunshine Coast.

Tim had an interview at a public school with an exceptional music program.

We went on a boat ride along the Noosa River.

When the sun set, the stars came out as huge and glowing as planes with their landing lights on coming in over the sea.

This part of the country spoke to me.

The water spoke. And the light.

I took the job and we moved.

I did not know then that I was moving to a state where my story had roots. Apartheid, that shadow of legislature that destroyed so many lives in South Africa for all of my life there, was modelled on the *Aboriginal Protection Act and Restriction of the Sale of Opium Act 1897* (these so-called protection acts are never about protection). This is what my Gamilaraay friend later told me.

I began to teach English in a small school.

Tim began high school in the coveted music program.

Paul got a job three hours away in Toowoomba and travelled ridiculous kilometres to do it. But there it was. After eighteen months we both had work.

I wondered about the understory in Australia. I could feel it, but I did not know anyone who could tell it to me.

Until I went to a conference in Alice Springs.

Arriving there was like travelling back to South Africa when I was a child.

I felt like I was in the old Northern Transvaal and apartheid was still in full force. The heaviness in the air. The red earth. The blindingly deep blue sky. The little black children running barefoot in the dust while the older generation sat in the shade of poinciana trees marking time, as if waiting for some madness in the air to pass.

In three heartbeats, I could feel it. Here was a story I knew. Dispossession.

Day one of the conference. In the afternoon, there was the screening of the movie *Kanyini*. A colleague said, if you want to know the understory of Australia, go watch it.

I came in a few minutes late and sat down in the hall. The film was narrated by Uncle Bob Randall, traditional custodian of Uluru and a member of the Stolen Generations.

After the film, he stood up. He was in the front row and introduced himself. Then he went to sit in a chair at the front of the room with his wife Barbara.

Any questions?

This elderly man with gentle eyes wore a white cowboy hat and carried a guitar with him. He was a legend – a tireless social activist, and the author of the song, 'Brown Skin Baby'.

He had been taken from his family at the age of about eight by a white policeman, and never saw his mother alive again. His story was the story of Australia. This was the one I knew was here, the one I had been missing.

Afterwards, I spoke to him. I told him I came from South Africa originally. I said, 'What can I do?'

He said, 'You're a teacher, and so you can share the message of *Kanyini* to everyone.'

He told me that once his people were so big. And so proud. That invaders came and took everything from him: his family, his connection to place, his spirituality, his language. Without those four elements of his life, without his *Kanyini*, he was nothing.

This was the beginning of my learning. I said, 'What can we teach the children?'

He said, 'You know, every Australian child has a right, *a right,* to know the stories of this land, to learn to be a custodian.'

So I promised that I would, when I got back to Queensland, seek out the people of that country who held the stories, and ask for their help to bring those stories and culture to the children I taught.

Tjilpi – Uncle Bob – told me about his silencing as a child, as a young man, as an older man. About the tearing of children from families. He was not classified as a human for half his life. He was *flora and fauna. Flora and fauna.* This beautiful man.

How do I begin, I wanted to know.

He said start here. Go walk on the land. Listen to it.

\*

The next day, I went to Simpson's Gap (Rungutjirpa). It used to be a place only for women.

A sacred place.

I walked through an ancient red and rust gorge between cathedral-high rocks of pink and orange and red that towered skyward on both sides.

Iron-oxide red dust coated my hands, crept under my fingernails. I scrambled and climbed. In the shadows, I saw the wrapper of a Subway sandwich. I clambered down and picked it up, folding it and putting it in my pocket.

*If you can get it out there. Tell our story. Share Kanyini with as many people as possible.*

I will, I thought.

The cool hard rock turned pink, flesh-like and I felt or maybe even tasted water on my tongue.

In a narrow part of the gorge, suddenly a pool appeared. It smelled ancient. The walls of the chasm reflected in the still water – an upside-down world as deep as the sky was high.

The sides of the chasm felt like they were pressing in on me.

I had been in Australia for a few years, but until this moment, I had felt like a surface-skimmer living superficially amidst the debris of so-called civilisation that lay scattered across the landscape: houses, roads, buildings, superimposed over a landscape that held something bigger, deeper – the oldest continuous culture on the planet and the stories and lives and wisdom beneath.

Tjilpi had also told me that while, so long ago, English emerged out of German and French and Latin, the sun poured down at midday onto his people. Here. Nearby. And even before that, while some ancient hand carved Egyptian, Demotic and Greek letters into the Rosetta Stone, people sat here and listened to the stories and knowledge of Elders being passed down. Long before Stonehenge, before the secret rituals of the Incas, before the carvings on the entrance to Tutankhamun's tomb, before the bushman cave paintings of mammoth elephants in Domboshawa in Zimbabwe that I once visited, Australia's first people were here.

These red rock walls were here while entire civilisations came and went.

The sounds of guns and English rushed over ancient whispers – and this was not so long ago.

I sat in that ancient sacred rock-womb and I thought about the piece of Subway sandwich wrapper, for example, in the crevices of what was once an area of sacred women's business – where anyone could walk now, and let rubbish fall.

By the time I left the gorge, it was sunk in shadows.

Back at the car park, there was a young man collecting rubbish, dropping chips packets and a pink flip-flop into a black plastic bag. Tourist litter was tumbling across a hundred thousand years of culture, stories, wisdom and traditions.

'Hi,' I said to him.

In the brief moment that our eyes met, I thought, in this young person lives a legacy of tens of thousands of years of – until invasion – unbroken story, and here he walks around wearing worn-out khaki shorts, his attention turned to the task of picking up tourist debris.

*

When I returned to the Sunshine Coast, I did what I promised. It took time. Eventually, I made friends.

Some of them were First Nations descendants from all over the country. They brought their stories into my life, and later into my classrooms.

Later even than that, Tjilpi moved to the Sunshine Coast with his family and he asked me to help him put together his children's stories.

For months we worked side by side. He talked. I typed. He read and reread what I wrote.

I learned more about his life. About the land. He gave me a small vial of red sand from Uluru and said, 'Welcome home.'

Students from my school illustrated his stories, and he was touched. That they were children, that they loved his stories, that was what mattered.

I spent so many hours by Tjilpi's side, listening to his words, his wisdom. If he could forgive the monstrous crimes committed against him by violent colonial hands, would I ever find it in me to stop raging *against?*

*

Paul eventually found a job at a university.

I began to realise that despite the tumultuous journey, we had not fallen into the hole I'd feared.

Our relationship had survived extreme periods of drought. Even in the desert. It managed to hold its own water when none fell from the sky. I hoped that one day, we would wake up to an explosion of desert blooms that expanded to the horizon in every direction – like the Namaqualand daisies in South Africa after a long-awaited spring storm.

*

We had not seen each other for a whole decade, you and I.

Tim was a teenager, and we'd been in Australia for years, when we went on our first trip to the UK to see Paul's mother, and to catch up with some long-lost friends.

Summer in London was about as warm as midwinter in Queensland. I remember the damp green of early summer in London, the low cloud and mist over Hampstead Heath as Paul and I walked and told Tim about our runaway stories: the last time we'd lived in London, we'd been so poor that even a baguette with basil and cheese was a luxury.

Ten years, I thought. Ten years since you and I said goodbye at midnight in Pendleton, Oregon.

I walked. I caught the underground. I crossed the misty street. I stood outside that monolith, the BBC, and stared at it, my heart pounding.

Paul and Tim were at a show in London and would join us later.

All my most admired journalists in the world worked here. Or from here.

I texted you. *I'm here.*

*Be there in 5!*

I waited. And then, through the glass door, you burst into the misty mid-morning.

I ran to you. We hugged. I cried.

'Oh my gosh, you haven't changed a bit!'

I could not believe it. I felt your magnificence. You'd become a giant. Against impossible odds, you had shot into the stratosphere – made it out from the desert to the pinnacle of wordsmithing reporters in London. Woman of words, of courage, telling the stories of others, giving voice to those without voice, fighting still at every step, the Big Bad Patriarch, but now with millions of viewers and listeners any day of the week and a Twitter account with tens of thousands of followers. While I wasn't looking, you'd become a magnificent force – a voice that was heard.

My heart ached and broke – with joy, but also with appreciation for what it had taken you to get there.

'Come in, let me show you around, introduce you to some people.'

I followed you into the maze. We passed studios and news rooms with hundreds of screens. This was one of your producers, this was another presenter. Did they know the journey you'd travelled to get here, I wondered?

Then we went upstairs onto the roof.

London traffic and the business of lives, far beneath us.

After a couple of hours, we went downstairs to the coffee shop – local haunt of BBC staff.

'Is that …?' I whispered to you, as famous TV personalities wafted in and out of the shop.

You nodded and smiled.

We grabbed our coffees and went to sit outside in the low cloud and the humid air. Soon after, Ahmed arrived.

Tim and Paul arrived.

We hadn't ever all met. We hugged each other.

'Ahmed, this is Tim, this is Paul, this is Shell!'

It was a moment in time – with the five of us altogether at the BBC cafe. For a few hours our narratives collided, tangled into one. Ahmed and Tim talked about flying and planes. In ten years …

Tim grew into a young man.

You'd been all over the world covering serious and dramatic events.

I'd found work and my books were being taken up by Australian and American publishers.

Ahmed worked at the BBC.

Paul was an academic and an author too.

'Jeez, have we all made it into the grown-up world?' I asked.

'Maybe,' you said.

'I still feel like a runaway, an escapee. Can I even trust that I've landed?'

*

I saw you for another afternoon. We stole moments of coffee and tea and pastries. There was a lot of laughter.

When I said goodbye, I already missed you. But we were experts at taking leave, however much it hurt.

We promised each other we'd find somewhere in the world to meet up again. 'I hope we won't have to wait another decade,' I said.

I walked away, caught the tube, bought a baguette at the train station and ate it standing in fine London drizzle and intermittent sunlight.

*

Back in Australia, I taught and wrote and chased the dream of safety and security I had been chasing in America. It finally materialised in Australia. I found an amazing literary agent and local publishers who wanted my work; I have been alongside inspiring writers at festivals and found a place where sometimes, I can say what matters to me in a democratic country.

I live in a community where people still don't have the keys to their front doors and go out leaving cars and houses unlocked.

With a government loan, Tim completed his commercial pilot's license.

We bought a house, sold it, and bought another one.

We finally arrived at a destination I once only imagined might exist.

Eventually flowers bloomed in the desert. Between us. Around us.

# 43.

# SHAIMAA

In 2014, I got my dream job and became the BBC's Pakistan correspondent. My first-ever foreign news deployment. Many warned me about how tough 'the gig' would be. And it was. I covered massacres, natural disasters, honour killings. But for me that was never the tough bit. The tough part was the fear and self-doubt. The imposter syndrome that hovered over me like a dark cloud. I followed in the foot-steps of journalism giants. A legacy of exellence I had to measure up to. I was away from Ahmed for a long time for the first time ever. And through it all I learned so much. I lived in a city and a country that I've grown to love and started reporting from Kabul in Afghanistan and was completely smitten by it. Despite the difficulties – professional and personal – reporting from Pakistan and Afghanistan will forever be a milestone in my life.

I also remember we wrote back and forth when I was there. I remember telling you that I needed a hobby. Still working on that, Shell!

# 44.

# SHELLEY

I've wondered a lot about how you do certain things: your reports on the acid burn victims and the amazing strength of these women ... it's like you get to highlight their story but then what happens? After the story what happens to them, to you? Does it go anywhere? Does someone take up arms against the perpetrators of these vile crimes? I want to know their stories, I want to hear about their lives ...

If I won the lottery, I would want to rescue all those girls ... give them all the medical help they would ever need ...

Likewise the families who lost their children in the school massacre that you covered. Each of those boys deserves a story, a space. And you were so compassionate as a reporter. I saw you for a nanosecond at the bedside of an injured boy on a BBC clip I think, and I swear I've never seen such kindness and empathy in any correspondent as you showed while you spoke to this poor, shocked boy. Your hands, the tilt of your head, the kindness on your face ... I had to look away and cry and wonder how you did it. It just seems that for you, these people's suffering is not just the next story. You're not just telling the story. You're bearing witness. It must come at a price. But then you have to squash it, move on. And because of who you are, I could imagine that suffering is part of your own story.

*

To my joy and disbelief, in 2019 you sent me a Facebook message: you'd landed the job as the Australia correspondent. You were going to be flying across the world. You'd be based in Sydney for two years. I called you as soon as I could.

'How often do you travel to Sydney, would you say?' you asked me on the phone.

'Easily four or five times a year!'

'That means I could come to the Sunshine Coast four or five times a year and it'd be like a monthly thing to look forward to!'

'I can't believe it! I've been waiting so long for this – having you literally around the corner!'

I don't know how it's possible that the idea of spending time with you reminds me of childhood. We were never children together, but you make me feel the same unbridled joy that has the flavour of being nine, of anticipating seeing a best friend after being separated for, say, the school holidays and wondering how you lived without them for so long.

But it wasn't going to be quite so easy.

You'd barely touched down when you were sent off to New Zealand to cover a volcanic eruption.

'Maybe as soon as I get back from New Zealand,' you said.

Then Australia caught on fire.

*

I stood at sunset on the edge of Lake Weyba with Paul and Tim and we watched a bushfire glow large on the other side of the water.

'Wow, that looks big,' I said.

'It's in Peregian Beach.'

'Can't be.'

'No, it is.'

We walked back to our house. An hour later, I noticed the sky outside my window had turned orange. I smelled smoke.

Once, when I was a child, a huge veld fire roared across the open grasslands next to our house. My parents had to run and wake people living in makeshift housing at the edge of the property. I stood there in horror and watched their shanty go up in a shower of exploding sparks and flames as we waited on the short grass near our house.

The memory came to life as the night grew heavy. I wanted to go and check the fire so we went back to the lake edge. Now the flames were visible above the water. The sky was orange with smoke. I felt panic. It was hard to breathe in so much smoke. In that moment I went from observer to participant. The fire was blowing in our direction.

I didn't sleep that night.

In the morning, we learned that Peregian Beach had been miraculously saved by the superhuman efforts of local firemen.

I drove through the town that day. You could see the evidence of human endeavour to save and preserve. Around me the air was thick. The national park on the left was the colour of charcoal. Trees were burnt. Smoke curled up from mounds of smouldering stumps. On the right, across that narrow road, houses stood as if stunned in the morning light. They had been licked by flames – and then saved by firemen with hoses. Only one had been destroyed. There was a garden fence partially burned and a gazebo deck roof corner that was black. Ash and debris lay everywhere, and the gasp of the wind blowing through, taking stock – the morning after.

*

That day marked the beginning of a fire season from hell. You were sent literally, into the flames, or close to them. You called me from regional NSW and told me it was like a war-zone.

The dream of going back and forth visiting each other faded.

More fires on the Sunshine Coast. Near us. We had to evacuate twice.

*

After the fires, twenty-eight years after we got married, Paul and I went on our honeymoon.

It had taken that long. To be in a place where we could say, we're here, we've reached square one. Let's have our honeymoon. We had not lost each other along the way.

We flew to the Whitsundays. We went snorkelling in the azure waters of the Great Barrier Reef and paid our respects to the world of wonder beneath the surface of the ocean.

Love broke through from the deep and found itself in the sunlight.

We talked about this long journey and said maybe wherever it was that we were trying to find when first we left Africa, had been found.

*

And then, as if there wasn't enough dramatic tension — a pandemic.

States locked down.

We talked on the phone. Weeks went by and I thought, this is it, we are not going to even get to see each other. You will spend two years in Australia and we'll be separated.

Until, one night, as things happen in fairytales, a secret door appeared. 'Borders are opening,' I said to you on the phone. 'Can you get here quick?'

'I'm booking my ticket,' you said.

*

It was evening. The sun had slipped below the horizon. On the road outside the house, I saw your silhouette. For a second I thought maybe I'd imagined it – that you couldn't be there, strolling towards me. There were streaks of burnt sunset in the sky behind you and then you saw me and we both started to run. You dropped your bag on the road. A car driving by swerved and nearly ran over it. I flung my arms around you and we jumped up and down and people strolling by on the road gave us a wide berth.

The next morning before dawn, you'd been up praying. We went to the beach. The sun poured over the horizon like a leaky red watercolour orb that spread into the sea. A seagull chased its mate across the sand. You did a voiceover for the chasing gull as she ran, head bent, trying to catch her partner. You pretended that this was what the bird was saying to her mate: 'Don't you walk away from me while I'm talking to you! Come here! Wait! Where are you going?'

I collapsed with laughter.

We drank coffee and sat on the beach until the sun began to burn our arms, the water turned translucent blue, and surfers began to pack up.

'It must be noon,' I said.

When I checked my phone it was only 9.30.

Time was elastic. We slowed it down as conversations moved us through our lives. 'Hey, I want to learn to surf,' you said.

So we went into a tourist shop and bought a boogie board.

I watched you turn into an eleven-year-old in ten seconds flat.

We threw ourselves into the waves as though we were children again.

You came out of the ocean like a bronzed sea spirit.

We ate pizza on a park bench overlooking the sea.

'This is honestly the best pizza I've ever eaten,' you said. 'What did they put in it? Maybe it's just that we're finally hanging out together.'

'No, it's beyond all deliciousness.'

The flavour though, was enhanced by the length of time we'd had to wait to be there together, just eating pizza, the most ordinary thing two friends could do – and yet for us, something extraordinary.

The next morning we walked on the beach again. Far. The sand was blinding bright. Waves shaped and battered the shoreline. The sun glittered on the water and refracted light danced in starbursts wherever we looked.

'So, I know that there's a two hundred dollar fine for getting caught naked in the not-naked part of beaches here,' I said. 'But when those two walkers have gone past, I'm going in. And if I get caught, it'll be worth it. What about you?'

You laughed and shook your head.

I threw off my tired old bikini. I had no more shits to give. Life was for the living.

I ran naked into the ocean. I body surfed. I didn't care if the whole world saw me and laughed. I was laughing too.

We were together for ten whole days – laughing, cooking, walking and being in the waves.

# 45.

# SHAIMAA

My dearest Shell, I'm sitting here at your dining table, the rain pouring outside, good-tired from swimming in the sea. Hair all frizzy but I don't care. You're just opposite me and I am in disbelief that we've managed to be in the same place at the same time doing this thing that we love most and that unites us. Writing. Together.

I imagined us writing in the same room. Talking about life and world events and how all that is external and political is also so visceral and personal.

This book is my first proper attempt at writing. I've always heard that it is an isolating, lonely endeavour. But this is not what it is for me. Having you as a writing partner has given my stories flow – it's also given them their most important reader: you.

I'm trying so hard to be present in this moment that we have together. We are looking out at the sunshine at your beautiful, freshly mowed garden.

I'm trying to breathe and practise gratitude because there's so much to be grateful for.

Is it me or have our reunions always happened during major world events so that the mere act of getting together feels like a high stakes endeavour!

Here we are writing ourselves back together, finding our way to each other.

Unlikely friends on the run. The Muslim and the Jew. The North and South African – together in their stories and their strife.

It's always a struggle for me to look back and see how far I've come. Looking back fills me with dread; it means I'm not looking forward. Or worse – that I'm standing still.

It's one of the things that frustrates my husband about me the most. 'How can you claim to be faithful and grateful, truly grateful, if you're not stopping to take stock of where you are and where you've been?' he asks.

I've never been able to explain it. I think the very nature of being a runaway is that your eyes are always on the way out; your inner compass points only to one direction. Forward.

Looking back is dangerous. It allows you to dwell in what has weighed you down. And yet, reading your beautiful words about coming together at the entrance of the BBC in London after more than a decade of not seeing each other made me look back in disbelief.

After all those years, we found each other. Again. You've travelled your distances and I mine – we've struggled, stumbled, forged new paths all inching our way towards one another.

I was now in the world. The world that you once told me had existed outside my constrained sphere.

I don't know if I ever really felt liberated being in London. From the moment I arrived, I strived to do something, to be someone, to find a place for myself and not get swallowed by the city's enormity. It was as though my gratitude for finally making it out of the Middle East manifested itself in relentless hard work to prove that I deserved this escape.

It's one thing to feel free. It's a whole different experience to share that freedom with someone who was touched by the same shadows of your confinement, someone who knows what it does to your spirit and what it takes to survive.

I use the word 'survive' very carefully. In my job, I've witnessed survival in its simplest and most splendid forms. I've met people who've survived war, rape, acid attacks and abusive homes, and what humbles and fascinates me every time is the quiet resolve by which these remarkable people tend to their physical and emotional wounds.

It also makes me wary of using the word 'survive' when I speak about my experience. I often ask myself why I feel so exhausted. What danger did I go through? What threats did I brush with before running away?

You, beautiful Shell, you ran away from literal daily danger. Your life, like many South Africans', was on the line every day just by virtue of living where you did.

For me, the threat was never to my life. It was always, however, a threat to my sense of being alive.

The irony and blessing for me if I'm being honest is that my escape came in the form of the thing I'd resisted for years. Marriage. I moved to London to be with my husband. But also, to find myself.

I realise now that we have that in common. You escaped with your husband too. You married the beautifully nerdy boy and made your way in the world and I know it wasn't easy.

I continue to be amazed by your tenacity and resilience. How you brave the world with so little and insist on moving forward even when it's hell bent on setting you back.

This particular ability of yours leaves me in awe. This refusal to allow your surroundings to stifle you even when you paid a high price getting there in the first place. Your relentlessness in searching for and finding your place in the world – on an actual map!

Seeing you in your house in the Sunshine Coast, seeing this life you've carved for yourself and your family through hard work and persistence, fills me with all kinds of joy. It seems that you've finally found your American Dream in Australia!

It's a privilege watching someone you love live their best life.

# 46.

# SHELLEY

**Exile**
Late stars, metallic through palm fronds
for aeons burning,
reflect and break in catchment ponds,
shift with our turning.
Beyond their lives they live as light
And ease my yearning
to race through territories of night
a fire returning.

I can only know that the word LOVE is a bigger concept than language can hold – but I hold you in it, as long as my heart lives and beyond that. I will not look away from the words unsaid, those that sit locked in the hearts of women living now, whose stories will never be told, whose voices will never be heard because they have been systematically silenced and oppressed.

Even though you and I are experts at taking leave of places and beloved people, it was so hard to say goodbye this time. I have to trust that we are good at what we do – being runaways. Distance, time, and our individual versions of continental drift have never been able to keep us apart.

# 47.

# SHAIMAA

I'm back in Sydney and our time together at your beautiful home on the Sunshine Coast now feels like a faraway dream. The only thing that makes it real is how full I am from being with you and feeling truly loved and seen.

I also realised that for the length of my stay with you I haven't once worried about my appearance. There was a certain levity during this last week. Particularly about what I wore. I was in my shorts, my tank top and my bathing suit most of the time and I didn't really give that a second thought.

In my strict aunties' and relatives' book that would mean that I'm so far down the dark path that I've lost track of what is right and wrong.

That thought also clings to every part of my existence. A question of whether what I'm doing is right or wrong. Of whether my choices are mine or different forms of resistance, tainted because they represent an act of pulling away from someone or something.

Resistance is so exhausting. It's another force robbing me from me.

That's why this week together was so healing. I wasn't defying anyone. I also wasn't trying to hide. For the first time in a long time, I just was.

What I wore was more a response to the weather and what we had planned for the day (which to my delight was mostly the beach), rather than making a statement of any kind.

I know this may seem inane to you but, believe me, I haven't felt that free and unburdened about what I wore since I was ten or eleven.

# 48.

# SHELLEY

I am in awe of your courage: the risk in saying what you're saying is real. The pain of the burdens you are compelled to carry is beyond my experience.

We can trace our stories back to Abraham. A study involving more than 1300 Arab and Jewish men from all over the world shows that the Y chromosome in Middle Eastern Arabs is barely distinguishable from that of Jews. There are shared ancestors and shared DNA. Our stories run together in words and blood. Bassel looked like my brothers because they share the same heritage.

I think of you rushing out of the sea, boogie board in hand, your sun-bronzed skin glistening like you were ready for some surfer girl ad, and on your face, the smile of an eleven-year-old girl. I have loved being with you. The joy I feel at being in the sea is doubled when we're in it side by side, waves beating us up, throwing us to the shore where we lie like children, forgetting the decades. No one looking at you would ever guess at the battles you have had to wage, at the things you carry in order to be there, being you, in the sea and sunshine. To me you are a goddess – you are YOU – the ultimate hero: you have made yourself out of the threads of fabric torn to pieces by the impossible situation of being born a certain gender, into a certain culture. You have made your way to the ranks of kick-arse foreign correspondent; you have been bruised, abused, harassed, and yet you wear your scars in the most incredible of ways: a warm, kind heart – able to joke and laugh and find humour and irony in everything. I loved it when you went flying with Tim a week ago – that baby you held on your lap in Qatar took you up in a plane and flew you over our house on the Sunshine Coast, and you came down beaming, high on life. Your smile was the smile of your immortal, unsquashable eleven-year-old self. I loved you hanging out with Tim watching Tik Tok videos, how you always listen with love to other people's stories about their struggles, and how you smile in a way that makes people feel your understanding for everyone's hardships – that burns away clouds. You have learned how to make yourself disappear, but you are profoundly visible now. Incredibly, you hold no bitterness. How is that possible?

I will always find a way back to you no matter how the world's chaos threatens to keep us apart.

Sometimes I feel guilt for what I see as incredible good fortune. The ability to have run away. Again and again and again.

I know I'm lucky. I have not had to do battle with my own essence to just be able to walk around in a swimsuit and wear tank tops.

I left my new sandals on the entrance to Sunshine Beach by accident on Friday evening.

It was a holiday weekend.

On Monday morning I returned. The sandals were still there. I put them on.

In South Africa, my shoes would have been gone in seconds.

Meanwhile in South Africa a few weeks ago, a pregnant woman, a mother of three, in labour in her own home, was shot dead by intruders. Her unborn baby could not be saved. A few days later, a woman who was eight months' pregnant was stabbed to death and found hanging from a tree.

Who does this? How is this my country of birth?

I know my running away does nothing to help.

There is rage and heartache that live there forever under my skin.

But here I am in a place where I can leave my shoes on the beach on Friday and pick them up again on Monday. There is a burden in this. How many South African women like me would have run away, given half a chance?

I live each minute with gratitude.

I've recently taken to imagining I am already eighty-five years old, and someone has suddenly given me my current self back and said, 'Well, how will you live your life now?' to which I reply: 'I'll suck the juice out of every moment – I will run naked into the sea without guilt. I will throw myself into the waves, eat ice cream before lunch and not give a shit who sees me wearing nothing at all.'

**For Shaimaa**
That moment when your clothing and what you wore
held no more weight
than a butterfly's wings
and your smile
took back the streets
the night
your eleven-year-old self

# 49.

# SHAIMAA

The irony and the beauty of this whole endeavour is that it was the most freeing thing that has happened to me at a time when I felt physically, and many times mentally, confined.

I've also owned my runaway status now. With cautious, almost bashful pride.

I'm a runaway.

I have not found my home yet. My attempts to escape have not ceased because the fear of being stuck or trapped endures.

And maybe this constant transience is my ultimate runaway goal – that life I've made in between cultures and contradictions – finding new places and honouring those I've been. Egypt, Qatar, UK, US, Pakistan, Afghanistan, Australia and all the other places that have shaped my life significantly in different ways.

Being a runaway for me is that ongoing quest for different experiences and challenges, to fight the seduction of comfort and conformity and yet to always be looking for home.

That word has changed meaning for me throughout the years. It's not one single location. It's all the places I've lived, the friendships and memories I've made. Home is you and me separating and reuniting through the decades and picking up where we left off.

Home is every single time I hug my husband when I'm back from a work trip, a meal that we have together.

It's all the tears when I say goodbye to him, my mother, my sister and her children. Home is my journey from our small flat in Alexandria to covering breaking news stories around the world. It's me looking at myself in the mirror and making a conscious decision to be kind to myself in that very moment, in that very place. Wherever I am, I'll always be a runaway ... but I also know I'll always be home.

# 50.

# SHELLEY

We know from fires and floods and pandemics that displacement can happen to anyone at any time without warning. Anyone can be a refugee in a heartbeat.

You and I ran from countries to escape flames of one kind or another.

Fire does not discriminate. Money, status and good standing mean nothing in the face of a wall of flame. Whether we are threatened by bullets or knives or bombs or fires, we humans will always run to get away, even if it's into the sea.

When I ran, I hoped it was towards safety, but there was so much desperation to escape that I couldn't be sure of what I was running towards.

We don't choose where we're born. Geography ends up being everything.

We traverse the territory of our stories instinctively – runaways making the tracks we have to travel to get away. The narratives don't conform to anything neat or elegant. One outflowing of self/words triggers the landslide of another. Our writing voices intersect and entangle and that liberates the story. Like a dream, it is a fluid, wild and unwieldy creation. By its nature – because it is ours – it resists being made into a predictable narrative. Our journeys are intricate and connected – like branches of a river delta – propelled, according to chaos theory, into a form that mirrors other forms found in nature: the force of word flow wears down and cuts through the sand of our lives, the debris, finding the softest places to course through.

Sometimes tributaries vanish into dry earth and others flow out of view; nature everywhere, does not favour the linear.

Even the line of our horizon is an illusion – in reality, part of a giant curve. On clear days, when the sea and sky are the same blue, the line separating earth from heaven vanishes and we float, suspended between two blues, surrealist figures that no one has thought of painting.

At different times in my life, I have squashed wild feet into painful shoes, squashed my body into jeans that are too tight, thinking, at *least these Levi's hide belly fat* (which of course is something to be ashamed of. Certainly not something to relish as a part of being beautiful, miraculous, feminine). And I know these are First World problems for those who have shoes and jeans and the means to buy them.

The narrative doesn't divide into neat portions that wrap themselves up and provide a tidy ending. There is discomfort here, as in all runaway journeys.

We have left things out.

Done a cost–benefit analysis.

How much can we, should we write?

Will this heal or harm us?

I sit with the silences and the white and black spaces; there are conversations we wanted to put in and decided to leave out; they are part of the journey – and they are not nothing.

This act of (re)creation of self with each other through story came unplanned, wove our lives together again, became a gift – incomplete, precious, a place to take refuge along the way.

# ACKNOWLEDGEMENTS

Thanks first to our incredible agent Sarah McKenzie for believing in us and our story.

Thank you wonderful people at Ultimo Press: Alex Craig, publisher extraordinaire, Robert Watkins, Emily Cook, Brigid Mullane, Alisa Ahmed, Katherine Rajwar and James Kellow for welcoming us and bringing our book to life. You are a dream publishing team in every way.

Thank you Christabella Designs for the striking cover.

From Shelley:
Thank you Paul Williams for being our first reader and for your constant encouragement and belief that this was an important story for guys too.

From Shaimaa:
To the BBC's Malcolm Balen, thank you for the time you took (mainly on your leave!) to cast your experienced eyes on our words. Your time and sound advice are highly appreciated.

And to my sister Shaza, who shared her own stories, braved the time difference between Australia and Canada staying up late at night after putting her kids to bed to reflect on our time in Doha. Thank you, sis!

From Shelley and Shaimaa:

To women who support other women – who push them forward and cheer them on and know that we can all rise together. To those who give time and space and listen to stories.

A special note of gratitude to the women whose lives have touched ours and whose stories live sometimes beneath and between our words.

We see you.

**Shelley Davidow** is the acclaimed author of forty-six books including recent international memoirs of displacement *Shadow Sisters* and *Whisperings in the Blood* (UQP, 2018; 2016). Her novel *In the Shadow of Inyangani* was nominated for the Macmillan/Picador Writers' Prize for Africa. Shelley holds a PhD in Creative Arts and is a senior lecturer in Education at the University of the Sunshine Coast.

**Shaimaa Khalil** is an award-winning journalist who has worked for the BBC for more than twelve years. She's currently the BBC's Australia correspondent. She has reported from Pakistan, Afghanistan and across the Middle East, covering some of the biggest stories of the last decade, including the Arab Spring, the military campaign to liberate Mosul, the 2016 US elections and Australia's 2019–2020 bushfires.